eat. work. shop.
new japanese design

Marcia IWATATE

foreword by
Sir Terence CONRAN

PERIPLUS

SECTION 1 SECTION 2 SECTION 3

CONTENTS

FOREWORD

How things have changed in Japan.

When I first visited Tokyo some thirty years ago there was very little evidence of contemporary design in either products, architecture or interiors. What I did see were beautiful traditional wood houses, beautiful handmade ceramics and lacquerware and a few buildings and interiors by Western architects and designers. There was very little that you could recognize as contemporary Japanese design.

This book admirably demonstrates just how dramatically things have changed. Japanese design has now become world class and the eyes of the design fraternity are now focused and fascinated by what is going on in Japan.

The really interesting thing for me is that designers have created a recognizable style that belongs to Japan, reflects its craftsmanship and culture and is not derivative of Western design. In a world that is becoming increasingly globalized this is very welcome indeed.

Long may it continue to flourish.

Terence Conran

Terence Conran

INTRODUCTION

Japan is rapidly becoming the world's next cultural superpower. In his influential essay, socio-political writer Douglas McGray termed Japan's recent drive to produce hip products its "Gross National Cool"—a phenomenon *Time Magazine* defined as "pop-culture production." The economic powerhouse of the 1980s has refocused her energies from mass production to design and popular culture, as the players in the new era of Japanese cool—street-fashion designers, independent filmmakers, indie record labels, artists of the "Super Flat" movement, art galleries, DJs, restaurateurs and interior designers—gradually gain international recognition.

The change first began in the early 1990s, when Japan's "Bubble Economy" collapsed. With massive budget cuts, the nation's designers were forced to re-evaluate the jarring landscape of huge, garish buildings left behind by the bubble generation, who aspired toward any and everything extravagant, Western and international. Japan's younger designers retaliated by returning to their roots—and began exploring traditional Japanese materials and architectural features, the use of abstract new shapes and textures, as well as the "zen" garden landscapes that are so quintessentially Japanese.

Young interior architects, working hand-in-hand with up-and-coming avant garde entrepreneurs, are today completely reshaping the basic concepts of how contemporary Japanese eat, work and shop. This new generation of businesspeople seized the opportunities that came with the economic downturn—as rental fees, construction costs and interest rates plummeted. Disillusioned with the false stability offered by employment in the large corporations of Japan Inc, they opted to establish their own businesses. These entrepreneurs capitalize on Japan's vibrant youth market and its fascination with newness and change, as well as the recent IT revolution—in partnership with a new generation of designers and architects—to redefine a national image that was once deeply rooted in the rigid conventions of the workplace. Unhindered by the barriers of tradition, the new Japan style has now become synonymous with youth, hip and cool culture.

This volume showcases seven of Japan's foremost interior architects, whose diverse styles reflect the eclectic tastes of contemporary Japan. Like all Japanese master craftsmen, they express their creative energy through fine detailing and complex finishes. This high level of crafts-manship is one reason why Japanese interior design is now state-of-the-art. Whereas in the past Japanese design trends swung from one extreme to the other—from thoroughly Western to old-style Japanese models—contemporary designers now mix international influences and traditional elements. Modern lighting and new technology are central to the designs, but at the same time, the imprint of traditional Japanese materials and aesthetic concepts is clearly seen. An example of this is the use of spatial intervals. In a traditional tea garden, the path to the teahouse was designed to help guests transcend their social back-ground before commencing the tea ceremony. The use of distance in many of the designs featured in this book is inspired by this traditional Japanese concept of transcendence. Another concept is to minimize demolition, even if it means integrating the less-than-aesthetic existing elements or oddities into the design. This sets the younger generation apart from many other Japanese designers.

The influences of fashion trends are seen throughout global society today. In the world of interior design and architecture, flexibility and changeability—qualities valued in the fashion industry—are now rated above monumentality, which used to be the primary measure of good building design. The interiors of many shops and restaurants in Japan have to be renovated frequently so that they reflect the ever-changing trends. To avoid having to demolish their own work so frequently, the designers in this volume have decided to base their work on personal ideals or abstractions that are relatively timeless—such as time, history, abandoned submarines, a childhood experience. These concepts are often discovered and developed through conversations and personal relationships between the designer and the client.

All seven designers share a fairly "analogue" approach to materials in this age of computer rendering and IT technology. It goes without saying that every designer is concerned with materials, textures and color but these designers have diligently pursued materials to a higher level—researching industrial processing methods that allow for radical applications of common materials and freedom in fabricating new forms. Some also frequent the workshops of traditional craftsmen, hoping to enlist their help in the design and production process, while others scour demolition sites for materials to recycle. Some of the designers have even traveled across foreign countries on foot in search of exotic handicrafts, and applied their patterns to imported, non-local material. This is a rather uncommon practice among Japanese designers but one that has been found to be—ironically perhaps—far more inexpensive than casting the patterns in Japan.

1

Yukio Hashimoto speaks of two elements that consistently intrigue him—one of them being the relationship between the past and future, and the other being nature. He speaks of clues to the future being concealed in past phenomena and in the laws of nature, and of design being an outcome of visual images coexisting in harmony with the elements of nature.

When asked what his design objectives are, Hashimoto says the Japanese garden is always on his mind. "The design is refined to the absolute detail yet holds room for imagination and spiritual contemplation. There is an infinite quality of strength and beauty—infinite, so to speak, because the garden's design can be interpreted in so many different ways other than the initial impression at first sight. Each time I see how beautifully the view of the garden contrasts with the overall view of the landscape, perfectly framed in the openings of the garden teahouse, I become acutely aware of the power of interior design.

"During a visit to the garden at Konchi-in Temple in Kyoto, the work of master Enshu Kobori, I noticed an extremely intriguing balance between the immaculately trimmed azaleas and an aged tree, so aged that at first glance it appeared dead. In comparison to the more acclaimed *wabi-sabi* (subdued) aesthetic style of the *karesansui* school —which usually showcases a dry garden with rocks representing elements such as falling water and mountain—this garden was incredibly stylish. The appearance of the garden had a futuristic rather than the anticipated traditional bent most Japanese gardens have.

"As I walked deeper into the garden, I came across a teahouse named Hasso Seki ('Eight Window Place'). My impression of the teahouse was that it was delicate and, for want of a better word, 'sharp.' This impression was probably created by the unconventional use of many windows. The visit was truly a profound experience for me and reinforced my recent interest in Japanese culture."

Hashimoto is infatuated with intricately carved glass columns— successively lined in a similar fashion as the columns found in the great corridors of Chinese monuments—the use of calligraphy as text and graphics, and materials such as lacquer, hand-crafted paper and gold leaf. He explores the design and detail elements from various vernacular and traditional craftwork, and combines them with modern materials and technology. His interest in these architectural elements and materials is expressed in the omnipresent abstractions of *senbon-goshi* (traditional latticework) in his designs. The relationship between past and future is another design concept seen in many of his projects, as is his love for the fine arts and computer graphics.

Recently involved in numerous overseas projects, Hashimoto admits to discovering new inspirations wherever his travels take him. However, he finds himself increasingly appreciating Japanese culture and its native artforms.

Yukio **HASHIMOTO**

Kamonka
Chinese Restaurant

1F Tameike Sanno ATT Bldg Annex
2-11-7 Akasaka
Minato-ku, Tokyo

480 m²

December 2002

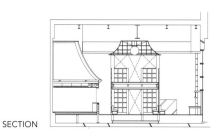

SECTION

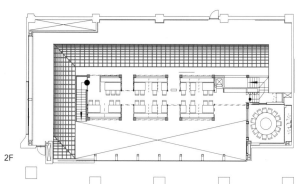

2F

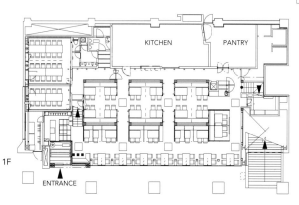

KITCHEN   PANTRY

1F

ENTRANCE

1

The success of this contemporary Chinese restaurant may be seen in the queue of customers who often stand in line for more than half an hour waiting for a table. The owners of Kamonka—which means "Gate to Appetizing Aromas" in Japanese—chose to open their new branch in the business district of Akasaka. The site was once occupied by a bank. Multiple internal structures were designed to appear like a phantom village emerging within the restaurant like a mirage, expressing what Hashimoto refers to as the "mysterious allure" of China. Passing through the large red gate, one is greeted at the entrance hall by an army of miniature Xian terracotta warriors buried under the tempered glass floor.

Sweeping monumental roofs cover the kitchen and banquet rooms surrounding three central "village houses." This stunning restaurant has a ceiling height of 10 meters. The kitchen roof (previous pages) is made of steel and acrylic-coated paper that has been silk-screened with a lattice motif. At left, bridges connect the upper floors of the "houses" to create a mezzanine dining area with a spectacular view of the majestic roof on one side and the view of the city on the other side. A collection of Chinese teapots is silhouetted against an illuminated wall at the entrance hall (below). The bird's eye view of the booth seats located in front of the "village houses" (left) displays magnificent acrylic light towers hand-carved with motifs from the Chinese Zodiac.

The banquet room (above left) is fabricated of reflective materials such as polished white granite, glass mirrors and high-gloss lacquer. The slick design stands in stark contrast to the decorative main dining area. The oversized porcelain vases and acrylic panels carved with calligraphy were hand-crafted in China. Seen above, full-scale terracotta warriors stand guard behind a steel grid, finished with the same rust-like varnish as the roofs, in a private banquet room on the second floor.

Daidaiya
Japanese Restaurant

1F Umeda Moko Bldg
1-16 Komatsubara-cho
Kita-ku, Osaka

335 m²

December 1999

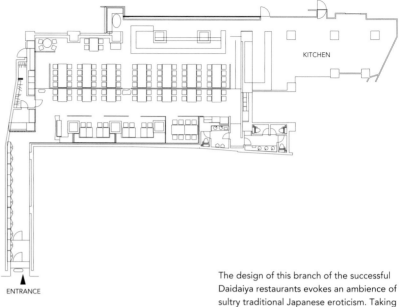

KITCHEN

ENTRANCE

The design of this branch of the successful Daidaiya restaurants evokes an ambience of sultry traditional Japanese eroticism. Taking his cue from the restaurant's location in the historic entertainment quarter of Osaka, Hashimoto redesigned the traditional *sen-bon-goshi* (traditional storefront wooden latticework) seen below in various materials throughout the restaurant, carefully controlling how the views within the restaurant were obscured or revealed, so as to create a contrast of virtual and physical images.

1

London-based design group Tomato created the restaurant logo on the door to the entrance, offering a view of the remarkably long alley (previous pages). Tempered glass panels set on garden gravel is dramatically accented with recessed red lighting. The latticework is repeated in the entrance—the wooden lattice (below) conceals closets—and the glass screens laminated with lines of red film (right). So successful is the erotic design that the famous photographer Araki, whose "flower works" are installed behind the counter on the left, once exclaimed that this restaurant reminded him of traditional Japanese concubine quarters. The massive maplewood counter and tables float above the sunken pits in the seating area with the unconventional black-lacquered *tatami* floor. The lavish vegetable display on the counter, installed with an open-refrigerated system, is a sight to whet appetites. The acrylic pipes and lighting effects create a virtual screen (below), dividing the room with the extended tables into a floor-seating area and chair-seating area behind the screen. Illuminated acrylic pipes (right), sandblasted with a ring motif, create an interesting distortion of view.

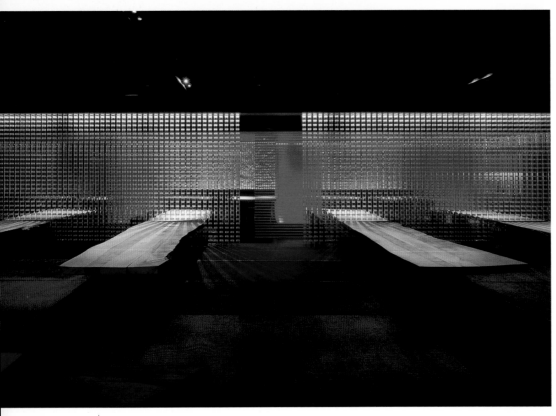

Lan-Ting
Chinese Restaurant

3F Grand Formosa Regent Hotel Taipei
41 Chung Shan N Rd Section 2
Taipei, 2TW, Taiwan

774 m²

July 2001

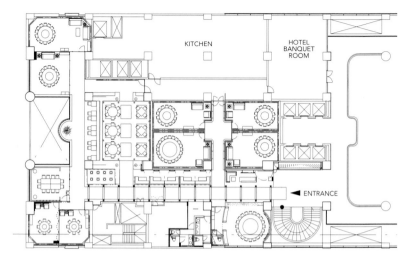

In his design brief for this upscale restaurant in Taipei's five-star Grand Formosa Regent Hotel, the company's president Stephen Pan asked that calligraphy be used as the central motif. This presented Hashimoto, who is an ardent admirer of the treasures in Taiwan's National Palace Museum, with the perfect opportunity to explore the various possibilities of linking China's rich culture with the future. Chinese characters, laser-cut in glass, were positioned between two glass panels and were illuminated by recessed lighting. These "floating" images (right) give the restaurant a futuristic feel.

1

The perforated porcelain pendants in the main dining area are reminiscent of Chinese lanterns (previous pages). Calligraphy is seen throughout the restaurant, although its presence is subtle and almost invisible—obscured behind sandblasted glass, or positioned to appear in and out of view from between the structural columns. The display area seen above is located at the end of a dramatic calligraphy-adorned passageway, showcasing an installation of ceramic bowls gently overflowing with water. The pump system is cleverly housed in mirror-finished stainless-steel cubes. A lacquered wooden latticework frames the glass panel covered with film-cut calligraphy and fluorescent-red acrylic (left) which Hashimoto hand-carried from Tokyo along with the sleek Lazy Susan and acrylic vases serving as the centerpiece in another private banquet room (right).

Gekka
Bar

41F Shiodome City Center
1-5-2 Higashi-shinbashi
Minato-ku, Tokyo

82 m²

April 2003

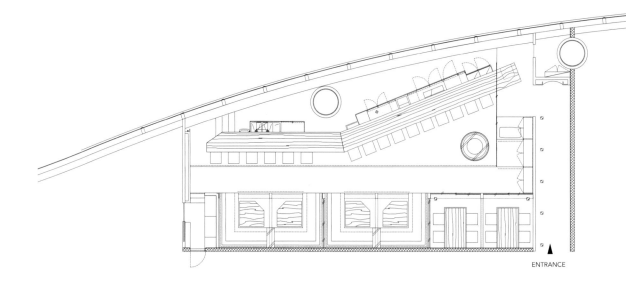

ENTRANCE

1

To Hashimoto, the designing of bars is a challenging conceptual exercise since the ambience and mood created can dramatically influence the experience and even the taste of the drinks themselves. This is why Hashimoto—who is fond of the occasional drink himself—believes in creating bars that are absolutely out of the ordinary. Located in a popular high-rise in Shiodome, a recent urban development near Ginza, the design concept for this exquisite bar was inspired by a scene from the movie *Gattaga*, which showed men in tailored suits entering a spaceship. Hashimoto envisioned the bar as a Japanese-style room in a spaceship and hence created "a Kyoto-style space floating in the sky"—an illusion produced by the juxtaposition of the glittering city view from the window and the traditional Japanese ambience within the bar. Before they enter the bar, customers remove their shoes at the end of the long entrance alley adorned with acrylic light pillars (left).

A sculpture (previous pages) by artist Seijiro Tsukamoto creates colorful and fantastic hologram-like images on the glass screen, using the reflection of ripples in a water basin created by droplets of *shochu*—a distilled vodka-like Japanese liquor—falling from a suspended bronze sphere. At the opposite end of the long bar counter (left), a copper light sculpture by the same artist casts interesting patterns on an acrylic disk, as light is reflected and refracted through faceted crystal glass. The ceiling is lined with a wire grid that is coated with high-tech photoluminescent paint, illuminated by blacklights to heighten the futuristic ambience. The sofa booths are furnished with sculptural tables designed with a folded edge, reminiscent of Japanese origami.

Oto Oto
Japanese Restaurant

1+2F Shinjuku Center Bldg Annex
1-25-1 Nishi-shinjuku
Shinjuku-ku, Tokyo

681 m²

October 2002

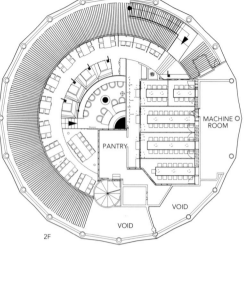

2F

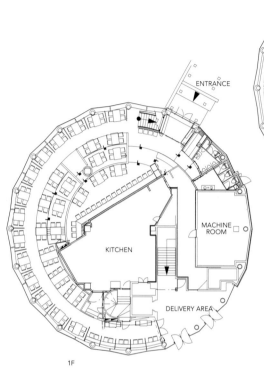

1F

This modern Japanese restaurant in the high-rise Shinjuku office district of Tokyo specializes in meals prepared by innovative chefs for diners nostalgic for home-cooked food which young Tokyoites living away from home rarely get to eat. After visiting the site, Hashimoto decided to take full advantage of the building's distinctive circular shape. Since the oversized glass facade gave little privacy from the street, he built another facade within the restaurant. The interior structure on the right is composed of a single element—rectangular steel pipes finished in sponge-stippled paint.

1

Hashimoto created the spectacular circular composition in the image of an opened *bangasa* (traditional oiled paper umbrella). Tiers of the lattice composition are dramatically accented with recessed lighting (right). Diners at the tables—which are arranged in a circular layout (left)—catch a glimpse of the central kitchen unit on the ground floor where Hashimoto chose a combination of *sabi-ishi* (granite with oxidized iron) and dark stained *nara* (Japanese oak) for the flooring. Tables in bamboo parquet, chairs in slick vinyl leather and pendant fixtures in hand-crafted paper and acrylic complete the look of the contemporary Japanese design.

On the second floor, true to the umbrella composition, the lattice design takes on a multi-layered appearance. The walls are decorated with *oya-ishi*, a soft volcanic rock indigenous to the eastern Utsunomiya region—which was especially favored by Frank Lloyd Wright for his projects in Japan—machine-detailed in a ribbed pattern. The counter seats are designed and placed so that dining couples can enjoy dynamic city views through the latticework. The lush, carpeted lounge area (above) is housed in a 90-degree wedge of the circular floor plan that completes the design with the central core of the umbrella. The furnishings in the lounge are upholstered in gold-striped fabric, adding a touch of extravagance.

After studying the client's merchandise, objectives and project site, Tsutomu Kurokawa proposes an architectural model, in many cases, after just a single meeting. "Many designers concern themselves with creating a space removed from daily life but I disagree with that concept. Retail design should provide a comfortable atmosphere. At the same time, it should say to the customer: This is an exciting place to shop. Each client and project has its own unique objectives so I try to understand those objectives and express them in my way—visualizing the design with merchandise and shoppers. I think that is creativity. And design to me is a very personal relationship with a client."

Kurokawa is inspired by visual images outside of the preconceived notions of design, and aims to produce work that is likewise unconventional. He is in perpetual pursuit of cutting-edge designs and materials not commonly used in the mainstream industry. His studio's name, Out Design, reflects his deep conviction.

Although renowned for his product designs, Kurokawa says that he is not a product designer, as the individual items he creates are designed with the context of his projects and the home in mind. He says, for example, "A refrigerator should be white or metallic, not red. It belongs in the kitchen where other objects are normally white or metallic. It is rare to find someone desiring a red refrigerator. Maybe this person has a red kitchen. Or maybe he or she likes Ferraris." Cost is another factor that is on Kurokawa's list of consideration. "One-offs produced for a specific project are costly as well as experimental so I search for manufacturers willing to put the designs into production economically." Technological advancement fascinates him. Although some products take years to develop, they can change society at an alarming rate. "For example, the solar battery forces us to be immediately conscious of ecological issues. Living in an urban environment in harmony with nature, that kind of imagination makes me happy."

Kurokawa expresses his concern about retail design being seen and treated as "fashion." He says, "The fashion industry has put itself in the predicament where styles become unwearable the following year. For interior design, this should not be the case. We are forced to build so much in Japan, where it is difficult for designers to incorporate existing architectural elements into new designs. Because of the amount of materials and resources spent on construction, I think it is wrong to scrap and build with the same frequency as fashion is altered—shops and other buildings should remain as they were built, if they are physically or financially fit to do so, of course." The energy of a space, he asserts, should be found in its design, which in turn should be centered around human activity. Kurokawa also believes that retail design should convey a personal message to society, and should not simply be just another visual product to be consumed commercially and, soon after, discarded.

Tsutomu **KUROKAWA**

Custo Barcelona
Boutique

1+2F AY Bldg
3-2-2 Kita-aoyama
Minato-ku, Tokyo

140 m²

October 2003

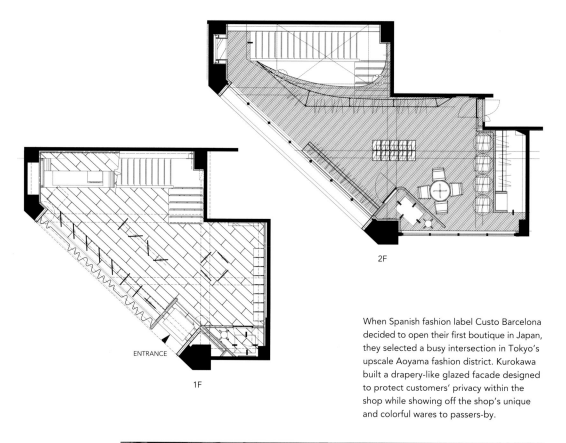

2F

ENTRANCE

1F

When Spanish fashion label Custo Barcelona decided to open their first boutique in Japan, they selected a busy intersection in Tokyo's upscale Aoyama fashion district. Kurokawa built a drapery-like glazed facade designed to protect customers' privacy within the shop while showing off the shop's unique and colorful wares to passers-by.

2

On the ground floor (previous pages), the garments on display seem to float in mid-air, prominently suspended on custom-cast fluorescent green acrylic pipes, much like in a gallery, where each item may be viewed individually. The boutique's sinuous facade was fabricated from four individual sections of curved glass (left), which act like a prism, distorting the view from either side of the glass. The acrylic hanger pipes are attached to steel pipes at a 90-degree angle (below). Custom-cast, mirror-finished stainless-steel shelves on the ground floor (right) create a dazzling array of reflected patterns.

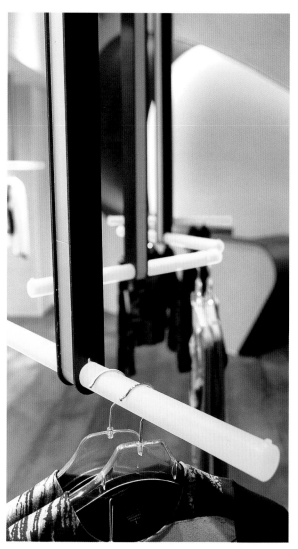

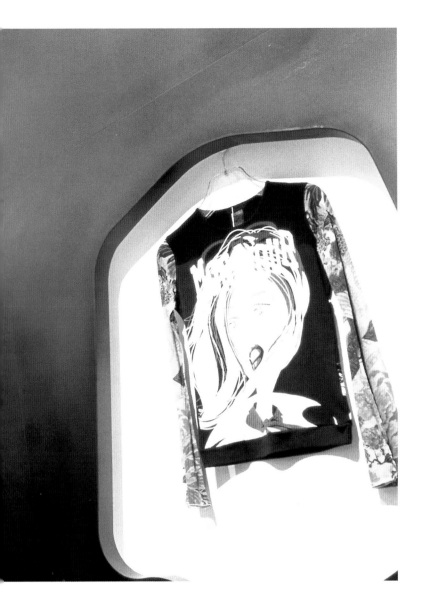

The second floor of the shop (above right) was designed to create a more intimate salon-like ambience for leisurely shopping, in contrast to the austere gallery below. Chrome-plated steel handrails seamlessly extend to form hanger pipes. Like the Spanish brand, the precious olive wood flooring is an import from Europe. As this was to become the company's flagship store in Japan, Kurokawa was asked to design a pressroom to launch new product lines. The panels at the back conceal wardrobes containing next season's collection, which rotate into view when turned. The sculptural staircase (above left) is clad in hexagonal mosaic tiles. Curved recesses in the oxidized steel wall behind the staircase, seen above, frame the garments as wearable art.

Jeanasis
Boutique

4-12-2 Minami-senba
Chuo-ku, Osaka

157 m²

December 2002

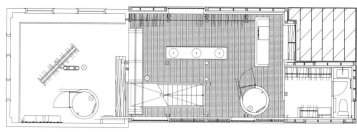

2F

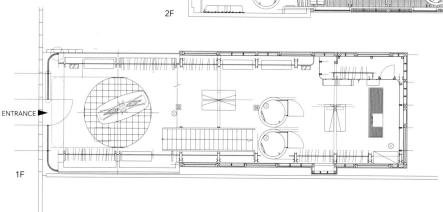

ENTRANCE ▶

1F

This sophisticated "no design" shop was created for Jeanasis—an iconoclastic Japanese label producing casual yet chic women's wear which epitomizes Japan's contemporary street culture. Against the grain of today's scrap-and-build age, where old shells are demolished or refinished to conceal their original form, Kurokawa is intrigued by the notion of grafting his design ideas onto a pre-existing environment. He also relishes the challenge of designing spaces with minimum alterations. For this project, he suggested that his clients locate their shop in an old building in Minami-senba, which is the trendy heart of Osaka. Kurokawa even dared to request his clients select a "peculiar" site, hoping that this might inspire an interesting design.

2

LOWRYS FARM

Hanger pipes (previous pages) fabricated from galvanized C- and H-beams serve to reinforce the original structure. A chandelier, custom designed from plastic beads, hangs from the ceiling. Mosaic tiles adorn the concrete floor like a rug inlaid in a pattern which Kurokawa considers a true classic even in the ever-changing world of fashion. The quirky ironing-board table is made of cast aluminum and Corian. When work on the project began, Kurokawa attempted to strip the building down to its original state. To his dismay, he found that it was difficult to determine what was original beneath the many layers of renovation work. The front half of what appeared to be the original facade was preserved and enclosed in a glazed museum-type showcase. On the left, the slick aluminum staircase leads to the second floor housing the more basic Lowry's Farm label also owned by the company. The wooden lattice in the background is part of the original building—it was the foundation for a former partitioning wall. The lattice and the wall tiles seen in the foreground were discovered during the demolition, and the post-and-beam structure (above) on the second floor is also a remnant of the original architecture. The cylindrical fitting rooms on both floors are clad with mosaic tiles in the checkered and striped patterns Kurokawa favors.

Adam et Rope
Boutique

1+2F Bera Bldg II
3-11-7 Ichiban-cho
Aoba-ku, Sendai

284 m²

September 2001

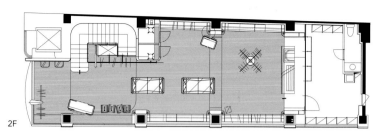

2F

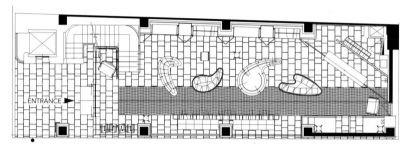

ENTRANCE ▶

1F

Adam et Rope, famous for their unique, eclectic selection of contemporary fashions, "dead-stock" vintage clothing, as well as international music and visual images, designs each of their boutiques around a distinctive theme. The concept for this branch in the eastern Japanese city of

Sendai revolves around a composition of curved forms and weathered textures, mimicking those of an abandoned zeppelin or submarine and reminiscent of childhood hide-outs. Behind the wood-framed automatic door of the entrance, this two-story shop offers merchandise for both sexes.

2

The aluminum wall (previous pages), steel railing and stairs have been painstakingly acid-oxidized and riveted to create a weathered texture. The stairs and railing follow the curved forms of submarine hardware. A painting entitled "The Little Prince" by artist Akira Uno hangs in the stairwell. The ground floor, seen from the cashier's desk surrounded by riveted aluminum (below) is designed to suggest an empty closet, and the image of finding the exact one amongst the clutter. In line with this idea, Kurokawa designed the fixtures in different shapes, materials and levels, placing them at various angles so as to create a cluttered ambience. The bridge (left) is designed to serve a dual function—it is both a window display and a hanger pipe within the store. Acrylic tubes (right) dispersed throughout the two floors are magnetically suspended from the ceiling, allowing them to be moved about freely.

The flooring on the second floor (left) is a collage of various pieces of recycled wood. Steel-and-glass showcases are mounted on casters for mobility, a feature that Kurokawa regularly incorporates into shop furnishings to accommodate ever-changing displays and fashion trends. A pair of headphones hangs nonchalantly from a hanger pipe in a corner of the shop, designated as a CD section. A sofa with a burnished brass frame, an original design in leather (above), adorns the second floor menswear area.

Sage de Cret
Boutique

6-4-14 Minami-aoyama
Minato-ku, Tokyo

66 m²

September 2002

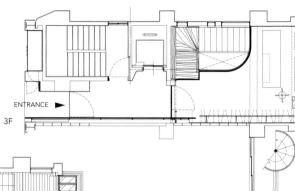

3F

ENTRANCE ▶

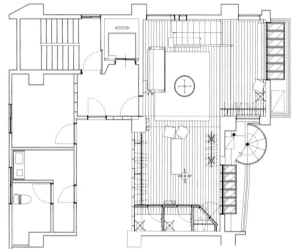

2F

This flagship boutique for Sage de Cret—the street-smart menswear label by Kimitoshi Chida, known for its functional zippers and snaps—is located in the upscale Aoyama district of Tokyo. Kurokawa is very fond of refurbishing old sites, which are often procured at the designer's request. Sage de Cret is yet another example of this design specialty. The slick furnishings are designed to provide a contrast with the raw surfaces of the original structure—sending a strong iconoclastic message to the scores of minimalist designs that have recently been constructed in the same trendy shopping area: Be Different.

2

When this former residential site was stripped of its many layers of renovation, multiple windows and ventilation openings were uncovered. Kurokawa decided to take full advantage of these as well as of the interesting weathered texture of the original concrete shell, and therefore minimized areas of new construction. The staircase (previous page), brackets for hanger pipes and furniture legs were all custom cast in aluminum. The carpet, custom woven in an original pattern, is placed as an "out design." Newly installed windows in the original openings (right) were laminated with a milky film to maximize natural light and obstruct the unsightly view of the shop's surroundings. The floor stand lamp is a Kurokawa product—a vivid green, solid acrylic ball housing light-emitting diode (LED) lamps, distributed by Daiko Electric. Below, the shop's entrance is paneled with fiberglass reinforced plastic (FRP) grating and teak louvers, allowing customers a glimpse of the original concrete shell.

Pinceau
Boutique

3F Seibu Department Store A-Annex
21-1 Udagawa-cho
Shibuya-ku, Tokyo

104 m²

February 2002

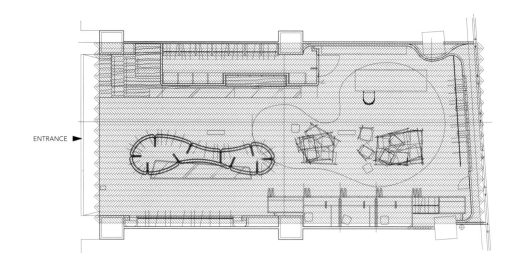

ENTRANCE ▶

The creators of Pinceau aim to add dashes of color to the customer's lifestyle—hence the name of the brand, which means "paint-brush" in French. Kurokawa designs each individual shop as if it were a different room in a home. This particular shop is located inside a department store in Shibuya—a sterile environment compared to the other branches that face streets. This shop was designed as the children's room, brimming with bright colors and toys. An overall view of the shop (below) from the department store corridor displays the vivid blues of the porcelain wall tiles and the hanger pipe.

2

The wooden louvers of fitting room doors and closets (previous pages) are painted in muted pastel colors, echoing the color of the carpet. The flooring is of assorted recycled wood. The theme is sustained with the toys and playful design of the storage cabinet (left). The desk, made of recycled wood, is paired with a funky checkered acrylic chair, a Kurokawa product distributed by Wazwiz. Display boxes (right) in clear acrylic are designed to resemble children's toy blocks and to accommodate the flexible display style. The carpet and hanger pipe (below) mimic the shapes of an artist's palette as well as the organic retro-Scandinavian forms that are found throughout the shop.

Akihito Fumita uses a concept and a meticulous method to reach abstraction and, in so doing, eliminates conventional connotations. The designer explains, "I employ words to help me view the subjective objectively, taking advantage of the slight discrepancy that occurs the very moment visual images are put into verbal context. Although words paralyze me at times, I find them to be the most effective means of separating visual images from the ambiguous thoughts that continue to float through my mind, and of forming these images into a more solid design concept. This verbalization spurs an input-and-output circuit in my thought process, as word structure requires consistency. I begin to search for a consistency between the visual images using this verbal filter—this is an extremely 'analog' process. After having done that, I then begin to delete the verbal expressions from the visual images, erasing the words which I think define the predictable."

Abstractions allow Fumita's design to be interpreted in numerous ways. He attempts to remove elements such as the vertical and horizontal as they merely represent the dimensions of what he calls the initial shell and a relationship with gravity. His use of curved, seamless horizons obscures the viewer's grasp of the boundaries between floor, wall and ceiling and this, combined with his signature use of recessed lighting, creates a futuristic and surrealistic ambience.

Fumita's work is also characterized by his inventive use of materials, as he has a fascination with discovering new applications for conventional materials contrary to their intended uses. For example, he may use urethane foam intended for insulation, Dia-Block children's play blocks, or thermal glass intended for exterior glazing for wall finishings or artificial marble intended for waterproof fittings, among other things. These materials are most often used in conjunction with creative lighting ideas, creating totally new appearances.

Fumita is also fond of transforming standard materials, such as stainless steel, through a multitude of industrial processing methods and techniques. These may include custom molding, vibration etching, perforation as well as embossing. These techniques allow him to manipulate not only the material's form and texture, but also to control the reflection or saturation of light in his designs.

Fumita is a good example of the practical artist, whose choice of materials is not only based on their beauty but also on functional considerations such as the material's cost and physical endurance. Of the desired effect of his creations, he says, "I do not intend to have my work interpreted as a direct message consisting of visual images—I find that a bit boring—it is far more exhilarating to anticipate how it might be experienced by people, and especially so if the designs are able to stir verbally inexpressible sensations that reverberate in society in some form or another."

Akihito **FUMITA**

Star Garden
Beauty Salon & Health Spa

1-5-4 Shouto
Shibuya-ku, Tokyo

1159 m²

April 2002

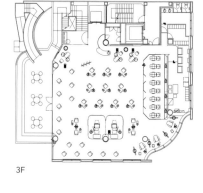

3F

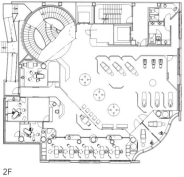

2F

ENTRANCE

1F

This is the flagship salon for Natural Body—a company that has perfected a form of massage it refers to as "hand relaxation." The art of hand relaxation stems from the Oriental belief that hands are the medium of the soul's expression and the source of all healing. The salon is housed in a three-story complex in the bustling Shibuya district along with six of the company's other businesses, which include a hair salon and a cosmetic dental clinic. Cushioned panels (below) enclose the hand-relaxation booths on the second floor. Circular sofas provide a place for customers to sit in the waiting area which serves the entire complex.

3

Doors leading to the consultation booths (previous pages) are cleverly tucked into a sinuous wall lining the corridor leading to the entrance of the dental clinic on the second floor. Flying saucer disks (left)—an illustration of Fumita's love for sci-fi objects—house lighting as well as ducting. Exclusive private styling rooms (above) are located in the center of the bustling third floor hairstyling salon. The curved walls (above right) are fabricated from heat-absorbing glass that the designer selected for its cool bluish tint. The recessed ceiling lights are reflected, casting interesting patterns on the glass. Fumita cleared the salon of all conventional fitted equipment (right). In its place, he introduced whimsical mirror stands and armchairs that the hairstylist or customer can move about freely, creating a more relaxed and friendly ambience than that of hair salons with a standard layout.

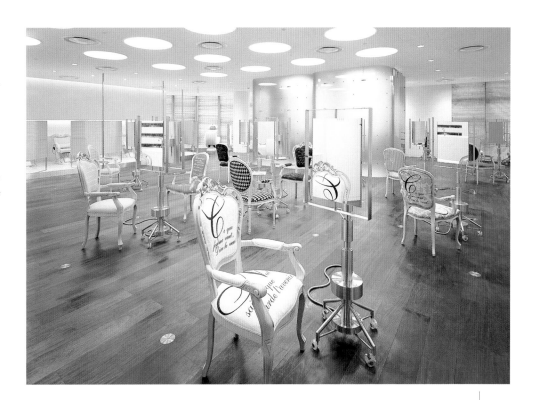

At the shampoo bar, freshly made shampoo is measured to the customer's specifications and sold in glass flasks. This innovation is seen below with the make-up corner in the foreground. Stainless tanks enclosed by a horseshoe counter store organic shampoo available in a variety of twenty fragrances. The design of the make-up mirror and chair continues the clinical theme of the ground floor—flexible tubing houses the electrical wiring for the curved fluorescent tube-lamps imbedded in the mirror. A special trolley (not shown) was designed for rolling make-up out to the customer. A stainless-metal tube set into the counter (left) not only guides each flask to the precise position but also catches extra drops of shampoo, showing an example of Fumita's eye for detail. A heat-absorbing glass shelf encloses the open end of the shampoo bar (right) and is fabricated with adhesive, eliminating the use of hardware. The reception counter is located behind the shelf.

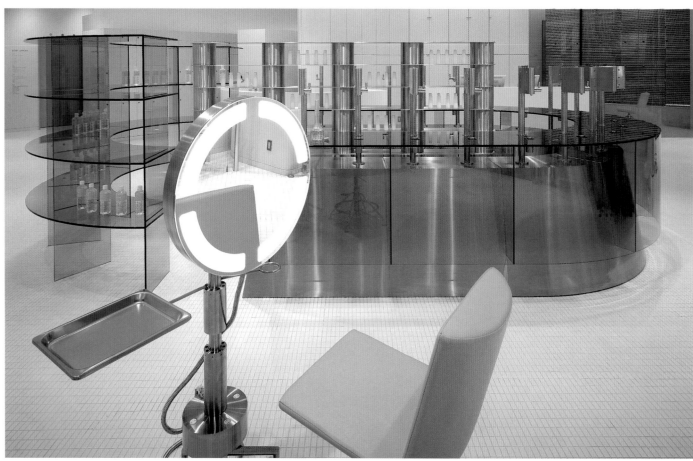

Nissan Gallery Ginza
Automobile Showroom

5-8-1 Ginza
Chuo-ku, Tokyo

292 m²

June 2001

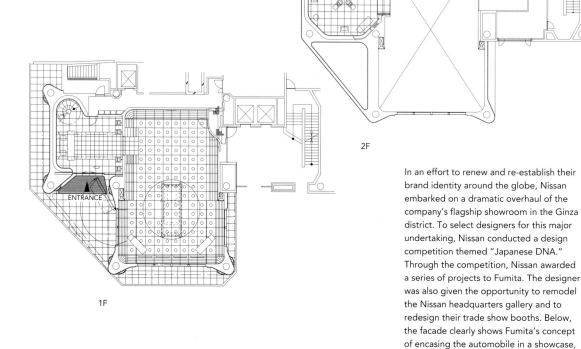

2F

1F

ENTRANCE

In an effort to renew and re-establish their brand identity around the globe, Nissan embarked on a dramatic overhaul of the company's flagship showroom in the Ginza district. To select designers for this major undertaking, Nissan conducted a design competition themed "Japanese DNA." Through the competition, Nissan awarded a series of projects to Fumita. The designer was also given the opportunity to remodel the Nissan headquarters gallery and to redesign their trade show booths. Below, the facade clearly shows Fumita's concept of encasing the automobile in a showcase, like a piece of precious jewelry in a box.

3

PRIVATE

The use of stainless steel, glass and plastic were key to this project for two reasons— these materials were personal favorites of the designer and he wanted to further maximize their application potential. The three materials also helped project a futuristic image. The sculptural staircase is a dramatic fixture in the entrance hall (previous pages) which is finished with the ribbed siding extending seamlessly from the exterior. The illuminated panel is of acrylic marble and the door is upholstered in cushion-padded PVC, heat-embossed with the same capsule pattern that is found on the marble and floor panels. Computer terminals, seen on the left, flank a ramp in the entrance hall, reminding visitors of HAL from the film *2001: A Space Odyssey*, and giving the impression of entering a spaceship. The terminals provide the latest corporate news on the second floor with its futuristic interior (below). The ribbed siding—seen at right— was inspired by the flowing image of raked sand in zen rock gardens, another one of Fumita's expressions of the theme Japanese DNA. The siding appears to be one single unit, but is actually composed of three different custom-made aluminum spandrel units—extrusion-molded, lost-wax molded and curved. Although Fumita usually uses metal for its appearance, aluminum was chosen in this case because it was the easiest material to fabricate and mold—the metallic appearance of the aluminum is lost under the white paint finish.

The stainless wall panels (above far left)—vibration etched to mimic the crepe surface of handmade Japanese paper—are integrated into the ceiling above the reception counter, which is made from a massive block of acrylic marble suspended above the floor on slender pillars. The colossal door next to the entrance (above left) facilitates the entry and removal of display automobiles. The recessed pits in the floor, enclosed in tempered glass, facilitate the change of lighting fixtures according to the weekend events.

The innovative circular turntable for display purposes not only rotates but also elevates during these events. Fumita's concept of brand identity is motivated by the interaction between the visitor and the physical presence of the automobile. The designer wanted to create an environment where the product is viewed in its purest form—the same way one would view the painstakingly orchestrated photographs in a catalogue. He was fully aware that the showroom automobile would reflect everything around it,

but decided to take up the challenge of fabricating the exhibition hall entirely in highly reflective stainless steel (above right). Fumita introduced many creative methods to remove as many distractions as possible. He did this by using vibration etching to minimize reflection, and punching perforations to minimize echoing. Curved edges and corners, signatures of Fumita's design, were yet another method that the designer used to remove the visual perimeters in the space around the automobile.

M-premier
Boutique

3F Nagoya Mitsukoshi Department Store
3-5-1 Sakae
Naka-ku, Nagoya

218 m²

March 2002

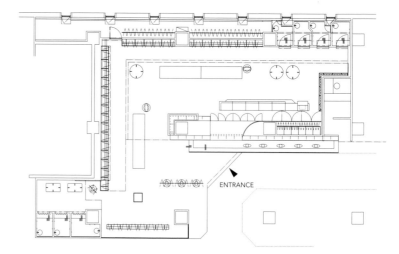

Fumita has been designing boutiques for the Osaka-based M-premier label of elegant contemporary women's wear ever since its inception. For this shop, which is located in a department store, the designer controlled the amount of light filtering through acrylic marble by varying the marble's thickness. This creates different shades of light, the central design element of the shop. Glimpses of the interior can be seen though openings in the light wall of the display window (right) from the outside. Sandblasted glass shelves (below) are recessed into the interior side of a marble light wall. Through clever lighting, the glass box serving as a cash table seems to float above its acrylic marble base.

3

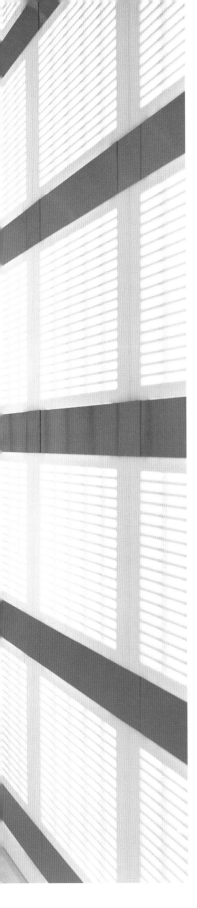

Hanger pipes in most of Fumita's designs are concealed—the designer hides the hangers so that the garments appear to float in mid-air. Here, as seen on the right, they are enclosed in glass boxes hanging from the ceiling. From the standpoint of the overall design, the furnishings take on an airy form independent of function or content. Machine-detailed in capsule-like indentations, the acrylic marble panels of the display window are joined by hairline-finished stainless-metal borders, and lit by recessed lighting, seen at left. The floor is made of stainless metal and illuminated sandblasted glass, and the combination of these materials further emphasizes the cool whiteness of the acrylic marble. The design detail of the recessed ceiling lights and of the ventilation louvers above the mirrored fitting rooms (above) follow the clean and crisp linear design of the boutique.

Ryuko Hasshin
Hair Salon

1F Makino Bldg
2-3-4 Toride
Toride, Ibaraki Prefecture

114 m²

February 2001

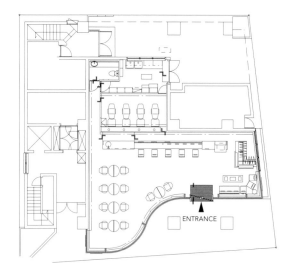

ENTRANCE

For this popular hair salon (whose name means "trend-setter") located in the provincial city of Toride, Fumita conceptualized a space that was "lighter than air." Each of the tables in the salon is designed with a circular recess fitted with a handle (left), allowing the table to be moved without touching the glass top. The interior of the salon is enlarged through the clever use of mirrors. Slight indentations and protrusions where the edges of the furniture intersect are seen throughout the salon, a common design motif in Fumita's work. Shown on the right, the illuminated counter edge intersects the hairline-finished stainless-metal block housing the cash desk. The cash register is concealed in the curved structure on the block.

3

Flanked by two symmetrical blocks, the illuminated counter (above left) projects the image of a linear line suspended in air. The glass box shelving unit mounted on the ceiling reinforces the airy design. Built-in stainless-metal units provide storage in the shampoo area located behind the wall. The counter in the waiting area (left) is fitted with two CD players for customers to use. The oversized entrance door seen above is inlaid with the shop's logo in acrylic, pivoting in either direction on a central hinge. Fumita cleverly set the door at an angle, and used recessed wall lighting to trick the eye into seeing a partially opened door, inviting passers-by to enter. Fumita handles the design of mirror fixtures in hairstyling salons with extreme sensitivity as their shape, size and position impact the overall design. For this salon, he decided to create an optical illusion of seeing one's reflection trapped inside a glass box. Clear glass panels—seen at right—were mounted on stainless-steel bases with the silvering of the mirror painstakingly applied on the inner side of the glass to produce a continuous flat surface.

Natural Body
Health Spa

B2F Namba City Main Bldg
5-1-60 Namba
Chuo-ku, Osaka

112 m²

April 1999

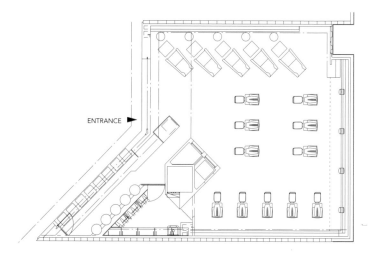

ENTRANCE ▶

Natural Body trains therapists at their Body College, which teaches that hands are the soul's principal means of expression, and the source of all healing. This health spa in a busy shopping complex in Osaka is owned by the same company as Star Garden (pages 64–69). Because Natural Body is a smaller version of the other health spas that Fumita has designed for the company, he has had to condense his design elements for the Osaka spa. The storefront (below) viewed from the corridor of the complex, leads directly to the main room. The spaceship-like room with its seamless shell is bathed in glowing light (right), relaxing the mind as one enters the almost other-worldly atmosphere. Portholes with recessed lighting serve to enhance the surreal ambience.

3

The seemingly seamless interior (right) is
actually fabricated from different materials,
cleverly lit by recessed lighting strategically
placed at transitional lines. Massage chairs
with alien "rabbit ears" are placed at even
intervals in the room. The customer strad-
dles one of these chairs and buries her face
between the "rabbit ears" as she receives
the therapeutic massage. Fumita designed
the unique chairs after much brainstorming
with the client about the functions they
need to provide. The striped wall in the
background seen at right and the storefront
are finished with alternating borders of
glossy and matt paint. The waiting area
houses a water bar where customers select
their preferred brand of bottled water.

Hisanobu Tsujimura's designs are all about paring the elements down to the absolute minimum—in keeping with the famous Mies van der Rohe doctrine: "Less is More." "The less you express, the more you can express. You confine the scope of the viewer's imagination by revealing all your intentions," says Tsuijimura, who shuns displaying his ego in his work. He strongly believes in creating only the central core of a design because its main function is to be inhabited, put to actual use, and evolving with those using the space. When asked if he is truly nonchalant about his design being altered if necessary, Tsujimura says that he is naturally partial to his original design, but tries not to be fixated by it. He believes that interior architecture should be designed with an attitude of tolerance for fluctuations and a capacity to encompass them. "Design concepts can be sustained regardless of change, if there is a mutual consensus between the owner and the designer."

Tsujimura lives and works in Kyoto, his birthplace. The distance from Tokyo, the urban center of Japan, has been beneficial for his design work, as it enables him to observe major design activities in the industry objectively. Clients come to his Kyoto office in anticipation of a Japanese-style design, and his hometown provides an environment that nurtures the instinct and sensibility necessary for the creation of those designs, something Tsujimura is grateful for.

"The concept of what constitutes 'Japanese style' is being transformed. Even though some elements of traditional architecture—such as the *cha-no-ma* (traditional living-room-cum-dining-room)—remain unchanged, I try to visualize its future form." Abstractions of vernacular symbols are often seen in his work. He replaces *rikyumado* (open bamboo windows fitted in tea ceremony rooms) with circular openings designed with steel grids, *shoji* (wooden latticed paper sliding doors) with light filters made of acrylic lined with paper, and the *fumi-ishi* (garden stepping stone) with a slab of rosewood mounted on an illuminated glass box. His effective use of shadow and filtered light reflects the aestheticism discussed in Junichiro Tanizaki's *Inei Raisan* (*In Praise of Shadows*). Light seems to be another building material for Tsujimura, who creates non-physical barriers with pools of shadow or large expanses of color.

Tsujimura strongly believes in recycling existing structures and has been renovating traditional houses in Kyoto, artfully transforming them into restaurants, retail spaces and residences long before this became a trendy practice. As he does so, he not only respects the beauty of traditional architecture, admires the patina of materials, and is mindful of the ecological aspects of preservation, he is also extremely conscientious about not wasting the client's resources.

Hisanobu **TSUJIMURA**

Cha Cha 2 Moon
Japanese Restaurant

2-6-26 Otemachi
Naka-ku, Hiroshima

165 m²

March 1998

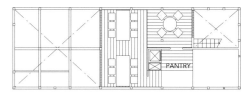

3F

2F

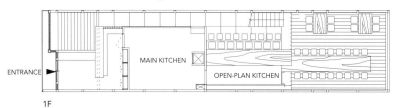

ENTRANCE ▶

MAIN KITCHEN

OPEN-PLAN KITCHEN

1F

The first and second Cha Cha restaurants serve modernized Kyoto *obanzai* cuisine, a sort of Japanese tapas. The two restaurants have contrasting and somewhat paradoxical design concepts. In the original restaurant, contemporary materials create a traditional atmosphere. In the second restaurant—shown here—traditional materials were used in a modern context. After scouting for a suitable location in Hiroshima city for their second branch, the client and Tsujimura finally settled on this former boarding house in Otemachi. Replacing the original facade, traditional latticework, which is repeated above the reception counter, creates the typical ambience of a Kyoto restaurant.

4

The building, constructed during the post-war rehabilitation program in the devastated city, is extremely modest. Tsujimura could have easily demolished it, but he decided to preserve it instead, as he not only valued the patina of the materials but also respected the history of the site.

The second floor dining area (previous pages) of the Otemachi branch appears to be in a highly traditional design but a closer look reveals Tsujimura's contemporary design—the floor is finished with *ryuku* tatami (borderless matting from Okinawa), the sliding doors are papered with hand-crafted paper printed with high-tech, light-sensitive ink, and the *rikyu mado* (an opening displaying the bamboo wattle of the earthen wall in tea ceremony rooms) is designed in steel. Pools of light accentuate a counter in the ground floor dining area (below left and right), illustrating Tsujimura's signature use of lighting, which here creates non-existing screens that enclose diners at each table in their own private world. A Noguchi lamp is placed in front of an earthen wall strewn with straw and tinted with ocher pigment, a traditional hand-plastering technique which involves skilled craftsmen and much time as the straw ferments, binding the earth to form a hard surface. A sole ramp supports the staircase (below) in a visually unobtrusive design, leading to the clear acrylic light walls (right) lined with hand-crafted paper.

The original post-and-beam structure of the third floor dining room area (left) has been preciously preserved to maintain the roots of the old building. Tsujimura stained the pinewood floor and latticework of the dining room in *kumezo* (a traditional Japanese stain made of iron oxidized pigment, persimmon lye and ash) to add patina to the newly installed materials. A view of the second floor—shown on the right—is seen through the smoke-stained bamboo lattice. The top of the dining tables (below) were beautifully finished with fabric varnished with multiple coats of *urushi* (natural lacquer from the sap of the *urushi* tree)—a disappearing craft—and mounted on slick modern alumite legs.

Cha Cha 3 Lotus
Japanese Restaurant

1-19 Nakamachi
Naka-ku, Hiroshima

202 m^2

August 2001

3F

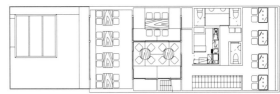

2F

KITCHEN

GARDEN

1F

◀ ENTRANCE

The lotus, symbolic flower of the Buddhist paradise, is central to the design concept for this third branch of the successful Cha Cha restaurants located in Hiroshima. Tsujimura discovered that the pattern in the fabric known as "Small Dot Pattern" by Charles and Ray Eames resembled lotus seeds, and so decided to use the pattern throughout the restaurant. In the second floor dining area (right) ottomans are upholstered in the Eames' signature textile.

4

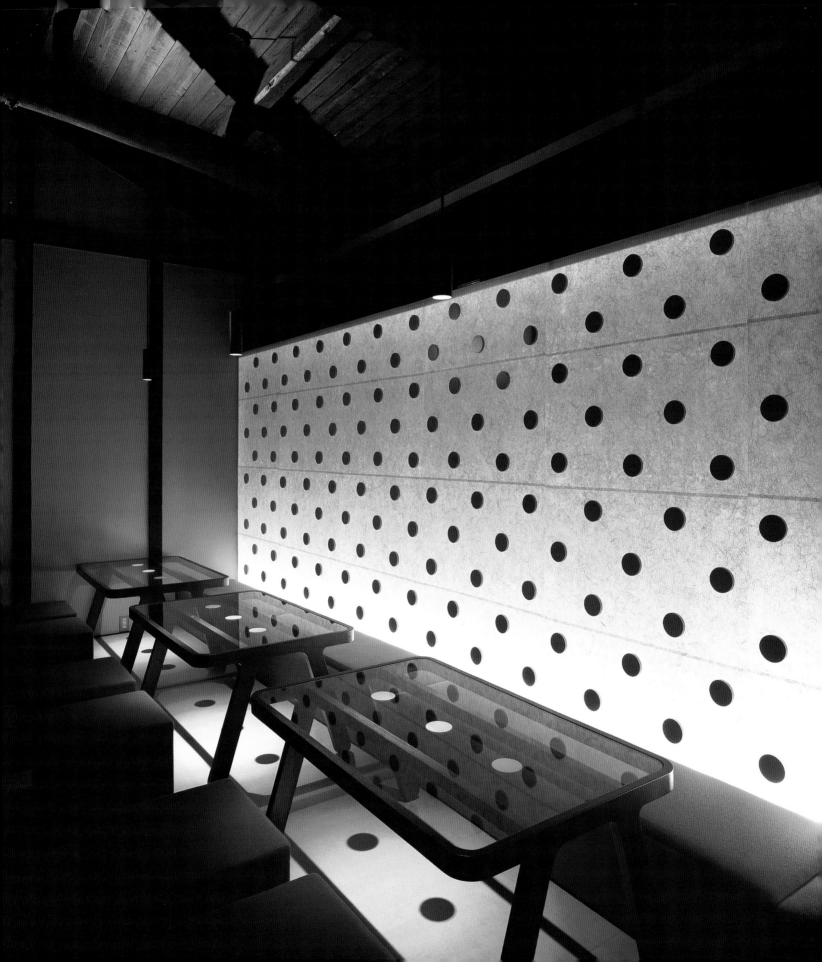

The dot motif (previous pages) is repeated on the glass table tops, casting patterns on the floor and on the light wall fabricated in clear acrylic lined with Japanese hand-crafted paper and laminated with medium density fiberboard (MDF) cut-outs. On the left, in the entrance hall, Tsujimura positioned a slab of rosewood mounted on an illuminated glass box, which is an abstraction of the stepping stone traditionally placed at the entrance of Japanese homes on which visitors remove their shoes. The sculptural staircase made of MDF and the handrail of conventional steel flat bars throw linear shadows on the wall, illustrating Tsujimura's clever use of low-cost materials and lighting. The polycarbonate pendant fixture installed in the staircase (above) is designed by Itamar Harari. The lively dot pattern greets customers behind the bar counter in the ground floor dining room (right).

Setsugekka
Members' Club & Bar

Sacra Bldg
Tomino-koji Nishi Kita Kado Sanjo-dori
Nakagyo-ku, Kyoto

148 m²

October 1994

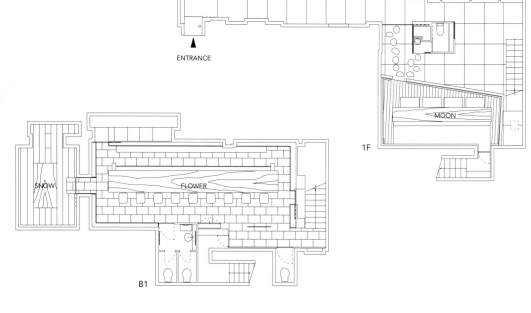

ENTRANCE

SNOW

FLOWER

MOON

1F

B1

Setsugekka, which means "Snow, Moon and Flower" is a members' club located in a building that was constructed in 1917, and once housed a bank. Setsugekka is divided into three rooms named after the components of the club's name. The rooms named Snow and Moon are restricted to members. Lavish banquets serving catered food—complete with traditional dance and song performances by *maiko* (young geisha-in-training)—are held in the private rooms of the club, a style of entertainment exclusive to the city of Kyoto. The third room, known as the Flower, serves as a basement bar. A light wall of clear acrylic lined with hand-crafted paper strewn with cotton fibers, bathes the Flower bar in a warm glow. The bar's wavy ceiling and orange bar stools add accents to the futuristic design.

4

The original granite wall of the bank (above) frames a window that has been sealed to create an alcove for the display of flower arrangements. At the end of the corridor, a staircase saturated in blue light leads to the basement bar. In the dark, mysterious entrance hall, stepping stones skim the surface of a pitch-black steel floor (above right), guiding the way to the Moon. The automated glass door, an abstracted garden gate, is decorated with a red lattice motif—which also acts as a safety measure to prevent collision. The fiber-lined linen wall creates a soothing, sheltered ambience in the Snow room. The chestnut wood appears to float, thanks to the clever use of lighting installed in a sunken pit (right top). Simple wall recesses house a flower arrangement and calligraphy scroll—Tsujimura's version of the *tokonoma* alcove—that completes the exclusive room in traditional style. The wall of the Moon is changed seasonally; here a wooden lattice-and-paper installation serves as a partition (right below). Linen fiber is strung in a different installation (above right). The client's appreciation of traditional Japanese culture is evident from the flower arrangements that can be seen throughout the club.

Kiss of Luminescence
Club & Bar

4F Apex Bldg
6-3 Tatemachi
Naka-ku, Hiroshima

235 m²

October 1997

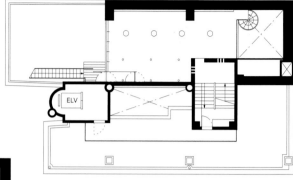

5F

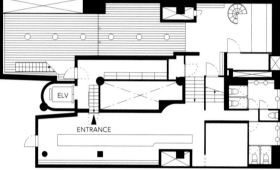

ENTRANCE

4F

This bar and weekend nightclub in the city of Hiroshima is located on the uppermost floors of three adjacent buildings, forming a maze of interwoven spaces. Because this business venture was an experiment for the client, Tsujimura aimed to lower the budget by using inexpensive, conventional materials and fabrication methods, minimal finish and by condensing many design elements.

4

"The merest distance before touch, the moment of bursting energy, repeated kisses of luminescence, the heartache of an inaccessible past"—these verbal images were constantly on Tsujimura's mind as he faced the drawing board. The images translated into indirect lighting, stark white passageways, yellow-green light walls and illuminated tables. The tables (previous pages) were inspired by the clione, a bioluminescent sea slug, and are fabricated of steel and acrylic tubing laminated with milky film to diffuse the light from fluorescent orange lamps. The tables are paired with classic Bertoia wire-basket chairs distributed by Knoll. The original wall of one of the buildings (right) illustrates the odd combination of spaces. A tangy orange wall further accentuated by orange lighting surrounds the spiral staircase (left) leading to the fifth floor, where the color is repeated for the DJ booth wall at the back of the weekend nightclub.

The clione-inspired tables (below) and unfinished pine flooring extend to a fourth floor terrace, uniting the spaces. A sublime yellowish green light wall is made from polycarbonate panels laminated with layers of fluorescent green acrylic and semi-transparent film. A narrow ledge in front of the light wall (right) provides extra space for clubbers to perch their drinks on crowded weekends.

Kiton
Boutique

Roppongi Hills Keyaki Street
6-12-2 Roppongi
Minato-ku, Tokyo

156 m²

April 2003

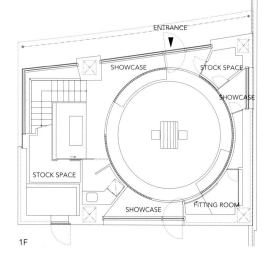

1F

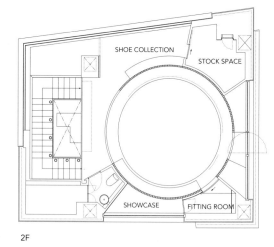

2F

The Italian label Kiton—renowned for its exclusive fabrics and exquisite tailoring—chose the newly opened Roppongi Hills complex as the site for their flagship shop in Japan. Tsujimura was commissioned to "Japanize" the universal design concept created by German firm BRT Architekten. The Japanese essence of Tsujimura's design is expressed in a vertically latticed cylinder intersecting the two floors. The lattice is fabricated in steel and clad with mirror-finish stainless steel and rosewood veneer. The stairwell is enclosed in a horizontally latticed cube. Furniture in the shop is made from the same material as the latticework. Together with the cylinder, the interior elements of the room form a coherent whole.

4

The fitting rooms, cashier and stock space are placed outside the cylinder. Below, the cashier's table is finished in rosewood and the floor parquet is of *sonokeling*, a type of Indonesian hardwood. The second floor retail space at right has a marble mosaic tiled floor, surrounded by an illuminated tempered glass circular frame laminated with semi-transparent film. The ceiling between the lattice and inner cylinder is finished in acrylic with recessed lighting, thus mirroring the floor design. Tsujimura based his concept on Kiton's exceptional tailoring and fabrics. Through the careful handling of material and form, the designer creates an environment that allows the feel of the garments to permeate the boutique and the customers' experience when they slip into a Kiton creation.

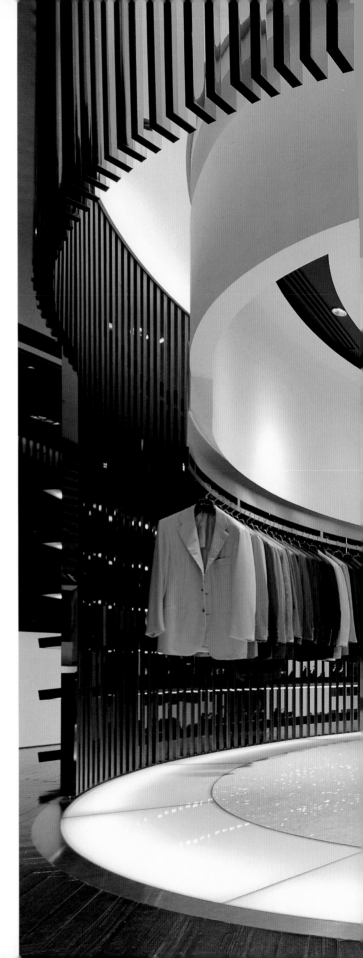

Is architecture dead? Yoshihiko Mamiya's question is not meant to provoke, but refers to the sense of alienation occurring in the urban landscapes of Japan in recent years. In a typical modern-day Japanese city, endless blocks of empty massive buildings, constructed to maximum scale of site capacity with extravagant materials, give way to obscure side streets around the corner, lined with sidewalk cafes thriving with activity regardless of time or day.

The roots of Mamiya's designs are found in the street culture of the '70s with the emergence of an area later referred to as Amerika Mura—or "American Town"—in Osaka City. America Mura was defined by the handmade wares, the funky shops operating from garages, and the tents loaded with new music, art and secondhand clothing—all of which were imported from America—and heralded the birth of a new youth culture in Japan. Mamiya's forays into Amerika Mura sparked his interest in design and inspired him to teach himself the art through

real-life experiences worldwide. As a designer of restaurants and retail spaces, he claims that he has no intention of designing form, which he views as rigid, and is more concerned with creating ambience. He does this by synthesizing elements such as the merchandise, the menu and the services provided with the displays and furniture. His work is a unique amalgam of the designer's personal experiences, history and culture as well as regional factors.

Mamiya strongly opposes the separation between exterior and interior spaces, a preference adopted by many of his contemporaries. Instead, the designer believes that "by obscuring the boundary lying between the exterior and interior, such that they interfere with each other, the silent exterior begins to narrate events happening within and beckons passers-by to enter."

Mamiya's former studio was a statement of his working principle. His studio was located in an area known as Minami-senba, historically a warehouse-and-office district on the outskirts of town. He designed a cutting-edge bookshop on the ground floor but blended it into the landscape and history of the area. This single shop triggered the birth of a hip new area with boutiques and cafés cropping up in former warehouses and offices.

Mamiya stresses the importance of "happening"—a key word in street culture—and talks about his ultimate goal as a designer. He says, "I believe that design should bring happiness to people. The city, with its architecture and interior spaces, can only begin to exist with human presence. Our environment should create a harmony between nature, society, architecture, fashion, art and culture. When sensitivity to people, place and time is juxtaposed with a new genre of stimulus, the design of a space is created. And more than anything, I would like my designs to conjure that indescribable joy that I myself experience from the sight of people enjoying themselves within that space."

Yoshihiko **MAMIYA**

G.B.Gafas
Optical Shop

2F E-ma
1-12-6 Umeda
Kita-ku, Osaka

104 m²

April 2002

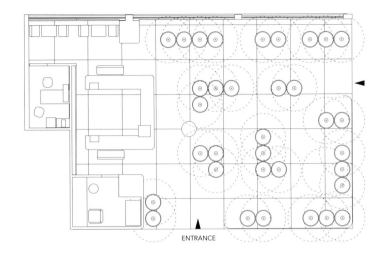

ENTRANCE

Unlike other stand-alone optical shops that Mamiya has designed for this company, G.B. Gafas is a shop within a shop, located in a popular fashion complex in Osaka, Japan's second largest city. To create a distinctive presence in the complex, Mamiya designed an expansive green tinted glass facade, and integrated the shop's logo with a screen of yellow dots made from yellow film. The dots —seen on the right—blur views within the shop, creating virtual images.

5

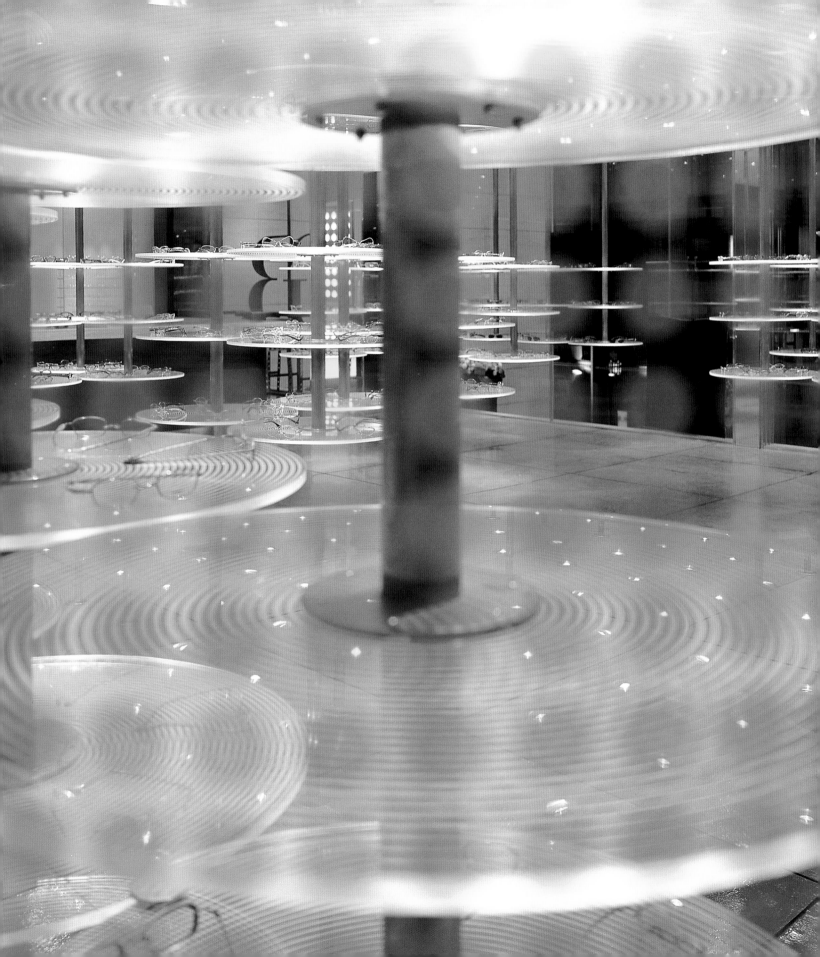

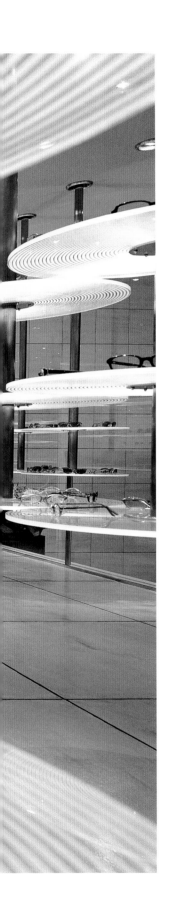

Circular fixtures (left) are fabricated in clear acrylic 10 mm thick, with grooved lines similar to those on a record. The fixtures appear to be illuminated from within, but are actually reflecting light from the ceiling downlights, a lighting effect created by adjusting the angles of the V-cut grooves. An eye-catching light wall of sandblasted glass is mounted on a yellow wall, and laminated with milky film to diffuse the light from the lamps recessed between the glass screen and wall. Mamiya's design concept of "floating" the wares in mid-air (below) takes its cue from the eyewear itself, which appears to float on the face. By creating a flow of traffic around the circumference of the fixtures, Mamiya attempted to stretch the customer's walking distances and time spent studying the eyewear in detail. Circular frames mirroring the theme in the ceiling house the downlights and fixture poles as well as climate control ducts above the counter.

/Scrub
Fusion Restaurant & Bar

1-9-11 Oyodo-minami
Kita-ku, Osaka

488 m²

June 1999

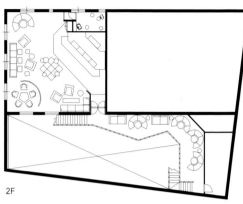

2F

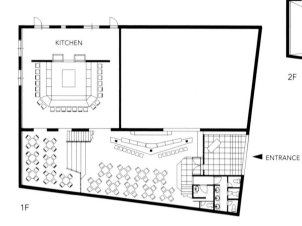

KITCHEN

◀ ENTRANCE

1F

The brainchild of a famous restaurant consultant, this fusion restaurant and bar is housed in a former lumberyard in downtown Osaka, and is frequented by celebrities and members of the television industry due to its proximity to a network station. Mamiya installed a new mezzanine, complete with teak walls, a kitchen and bar counter in the lower story (below) and a lounge area in the story above, while basically leaving the former structure intact. The original truss beams and ceiling are visible from the mezzanine (right), above the black leather bar counter.

5

Seen on the left, generic wall sconces were chrome-plated to accentuate the recycled brick wall behind the bar counter on the ground floor, fitted with vintage-style porcelain beer taps. The walls of the original wooden structure have been covered with grids (below) adorned with painted steel squares highlighted with recessed lighting. Tables in the ground floor restaurant are paired with café chairs designed by Aldo Cibic. The horseshoe counter that surrounds the open-plan kitchen is enclosed in a box-like structure backed by panels, seen at right, featuring the work of graphic design team Style. The staircase adjacent to the panels leads to a mezzanine lounge.

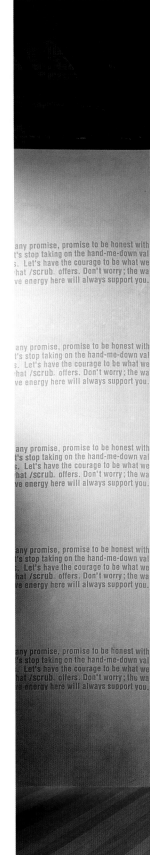

EXPERIENCE
IS BETTER THAN
LEARNING WITHOUT

100% Relax

The VIP section of the mezzanine lounge (left) is enclosed by a translucent curtain and a screen of mirrored acrylic disks. A funky chandelier, fashioned from ordinary glass ball fixtures that are simply bunched together, and classic deco Rene Herbst chairs adorn the VIP section. The lounge area (above) furnished with the custom-designed sofas, shadow lamps designed by Marcel Wanders and pony-skin chairs designed by Le Corbusier (not shown) illustrate Mamiya's talent for mixing designs.

Muse
Gallery, Bar & Café

1-21-7 Minami-horie
Nishi-ku, Osaka

216 m²

October 1998

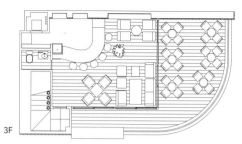

3F

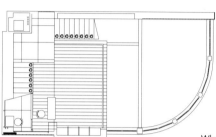

2F

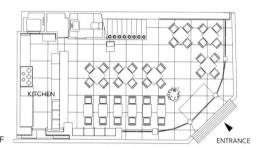

KITCHEN

1F

ENTRANCE

When Mamiya and his client visited the empty corner lot in Minami-horie in western Osaka prior to construction, they were advised to take the ground floor of the seven-story building planned for the site. The designer diligently persuaded the owner of the lot to replace the pre-existing building plan with one he proposed, which he promised would reduce the cost of construction as well as provide an opportunity to invigorate the area. The owner finally agreed. A curved building was designed for the site, a three-story museum-like structure housing a café (right), gallery and bar.

5

This landmark building triggered an near-overnight transformation of the area, and prompted the rapid establishment of hip cafés, trendy boutiques and progressive galleries introducing young artists and new art movements. Crossbeams (previous pages) supporting the structure and mezzanine provide interesting visual elements in the stark space. Massive steel sculptures (left and above) by artist Maki Taniguchi are found in the ground floor café and in the mezzanine gallery. The café furniture is designed by Truck, an Osaka-based furniture studio, and the planter, designed by Mamiya, is of patinated copper. The mezzanine gallery is finished in whitewashed pine.

A large painting by Akihiko Harada (left) adorns the entrance wall finished in *apiton*, a tropical hardwood, and potted plants on the staircase add a touch of warmth to the bare concrete floor. The bar on the third floor (right) is wrapped by a large terrace for alfresco seating on warm evenings, and its custom-designed furniture creates an intimate salon-like ambience.

Decora
Optical Shop

1F Sannomiya Sanshu Kaikan
2-4-4 Sannomiya-cho
Chuo-ku, Kobe

149 m²

December 1999

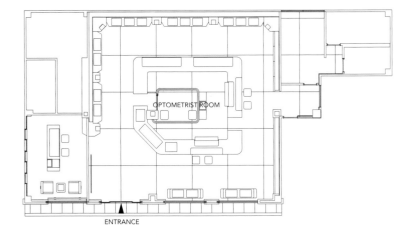

OPTOMETRIST ROOM

ENTRANCE

The infrastructure of the city of Kobe, located to the west of Osaka, was devastated in 1995 by a massive earthquake. The city was restored to life gradually as new street shops began to open. Mamiya designed this shop, the third in the line of shops owned by the company that created G.B. Gafas (pages 116–119) with the aim of brightening the Kobe cityscape. In order to achieve his goal, Mamiya installed many illuminated fixtures, four large windows to maximize the lighting from within the shop, and a line of red LED lamps creating a border, as shown below. The shop's new facade was finished with a silicon emulsion stucco.

5

Like G.B. Gafas, Decora specializes in optical wear. Spectacle frames appear to hover in circular display cases (previous pages) of yellow painted steel, illuminated by yellow lighting, and recessed into the aluminum-paneled wall. A counter top is finished in high-gloss urethane, which reflects the yellow cases. Sculptural mirrors designed in mirror-finish stainless steel add an artistic touch. Milky white slabs of acrylic on the counter tops and display tables are lined with diagonal ridges to display the optical wear (above). The optometrist's room is located behind the circle-etched glazed wall. In another area of the shop, a classic display cabinet fashioned from teak features titanium-framed eyewear exclusive to this shop (above left). Plush armchairs by Thibult Desombre adorn the carpeted area.

Higashi
French Restaurant

4-4-5 Minami-kyuhoji
Chuo-ku, Osaka

194 m²

August 2002

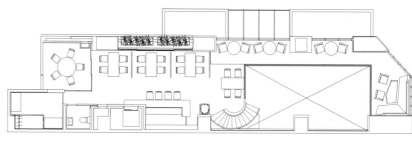

2F

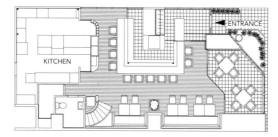

ENTRANCE

KITCHEN

1F

The idea of opening this retro-style French restaurant in Minami-senba, the trendy heart of Osaka, was sparked by a reunion with a former client whom Mamiya had not seen in fifteen years. The design concept for the restaurant revolved around recreating the essence of postwar Showa westernization through images of the supper club, an omnipresent fixture of the early '60s which the client frequented in his youth. In this nostalgic atmosphere, diners on the mezzanine level overlooking the ground floor can almost hear the live music and dancing that used to be found in such clubs.

5

Retro-style chandeliers in milky acrylic and steel (previous pages), curved walls in black cherry veneer, and booth seats upholstered in horsehair fabric are reminiscent of supper clubs of the '60s. The counter chairs were designed with seats covered in woven water-buffalo hide. The sentimental red wall, wrought-iron screens, and individual table lamps in the mezzanine dining area (above) illustrate Mamiya's forte in creating ambiences. A curved bench seat (left) repeats the rounded forms of the ground floor walls. A detailed view of the wrought-iron screen on the right shows that it is actually made of welded circles sliced from steel pipes.

Ichiro Sato believes that designing each space represents a strong act of volition and determination. "One needs to have a clear objective, to make a firm resolution, to implement accurately, to maintain an indefatigable perseverance, and to fuse all these efforts into a concrete visual form. It goes without saying that one must either resolve the conflicting elements arising from various constraints, or turn them to one's benefit as the design work progresses. Ambiguities that arise from the conditions set at the beginning of each project must be clarified and deleted through bold decisions. I believe that this working process and persuasiveness on the part of the designer becomes the guiding light in creating an articulate design for a commercial project —for the client, the contractors and myself alike."

Sato approaches each project by first familiarizing himself with the client's objectives. Factors such as site capacity, cost and location as well as the menu, merchandise and services to be offered by the restau-

rant or shop naturally have a direct influence on the design. Sato often incorporates old materials recycled from demolished traditional houses—such as structural wooden beams, *ranma* (decorative open screens above sliding doors), *byobu* (paneled screens), ship's timber and antiques into his contemporary designs. For example, in one restaurant project, the positioning of a stone lantern was carefully calculated to overlap with the high-tech LED-illuminated roller coaster in the background.

Sato often seems to be creating a stage setting for the elements that are the mainstay of a restaurant or retail shop. Another quality demonstrated in Sato's work is entertainment value, which he provides through the addition of some over-the-top details. An ambience of nostalgia, quirkiness, drama and humor is apparent in many of his designs. In one memorable example, the installation of pig icons set the theme for a restaurant which specializes in pork dishes made with free-range pork from the client's farms.

Sato is also known for undertaking renovations and modernizing grande-dames of the past that are threatened with complete demolition. He has successfully re-created a renowned traditional restaurant in Kyoto and old banquet establishments in both Kobe and Tokyo, transforming them into trendy restaurants on minimal budgets by the optimal use of the existing traditional architecture. These projects in turn have inspired him to reconstruct details of traditional architecture in completely new sites.

So what does Sato mean by a strong act of volition? He feels that all design is inspired by a sensitivity that one accumulates and stores over time, and an aesthetic sense which is refined and substantiated through experiences. He is referring, so to speak, of life itself. "This is why there is a clear distinction between the works of each individual designer. And actually, it is of paramount importance that such differences exist."

Ichiro **SATO**

Tontokoton
Japanese Restaurant

B1F Active Roppongi Bldg
1-2-3 Nishi-azabu
Minato-ku, Tokyo

205 m²

July 2002

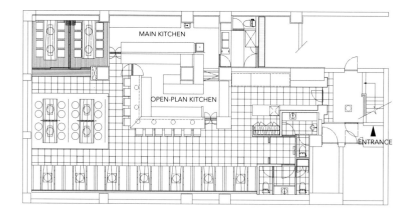

Located in Nishi-azabu, one of Tokyo's popular restaurant districts, this restaurant specializes in Korean-style barbecued free-range pork produced by the farmers who cooperatively own this restaurant. The name of the restaurant was lovingly composed from Japanese storybook phrases meaning "light-footed" and "pig." The star of this venue adorns an entrance door—seen on the right—made of luxurious *bubinga*, an African hardwood. Wooden plaques bear the name of the farmer supplying the pork for the evening. Shown below, the mainstay of this restaurant is showcased in a glazed refrigerator in the open-plan kitchen.

6

豚肉料理專門店

本日の生産者

石井夫妻

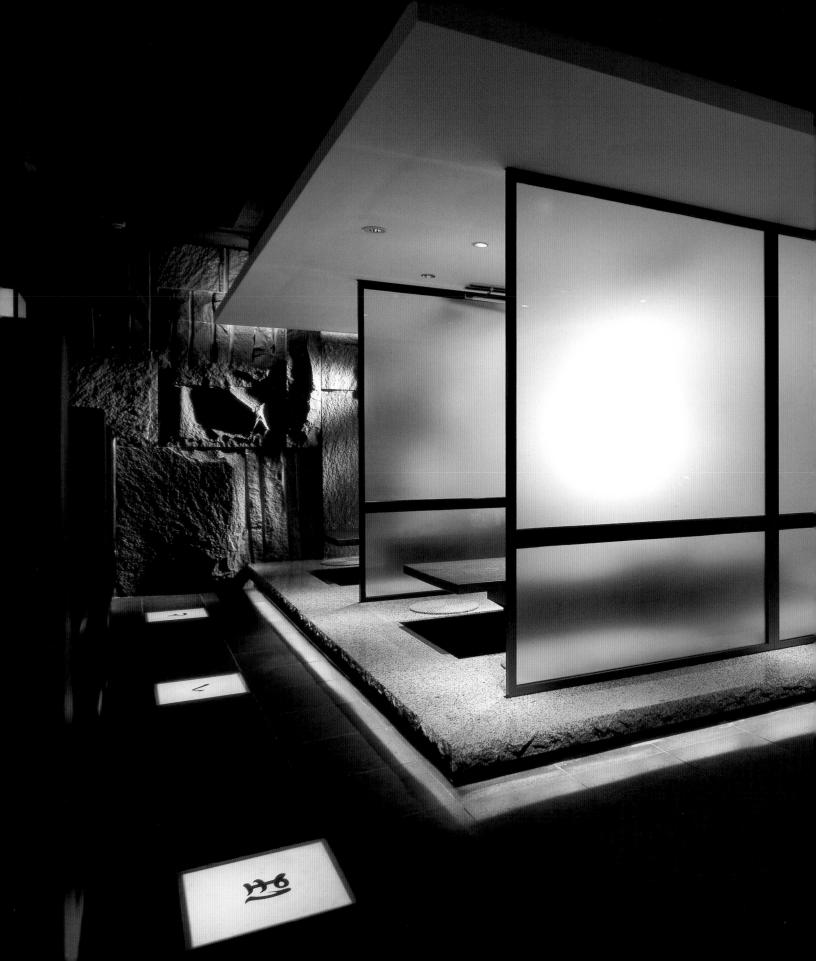

Semi-private dining rooms (left) are elevated on massive slabs of granite with fractured edges—the surface is polished to a smooth finish and warmed with floor heating. Sleek *shoji* screens are fashioned from sandblasted glass and steel. Sato often suspends partial ceilings in a skeleton frame to recess lighting and conceal climate-control machinery. Long dining tables, like the one seen above, are made from *bubinga* wood, and fitted with barbecue grills and a sophisticated ventilation system designed to absorb the barbecue fumes from below the tables. The dramatic sculptural stone walls and granite slab floors were inspired by a visit to a quarry located near one of the pig farms.

Sato dotingly dispersed pig icons throughout the slick, contemporary restaurant. The lighting fixtures suspended above the booth seats conceal ventilation hoods seen above. Table numbers are denoted by individual characters of the Japanese *hiragana* alphabet (right) backlit on recessed floor lights, another of Sato's playful ideas.

En
Japanese Restaurant

42F Shiodome City Center
1-5-2 Higashi-shinbashi
Minato-ku, Tokyo

624 m²

April 2003

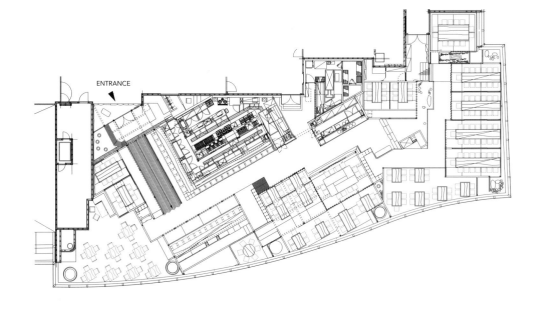

ENTRANCE

When Sato first laid eyes on this mammoth site on the 42nd floor of a monumental glass tower in Shiodome, he thought it resembled "a large piece of Mother Earth suspended in the sky." Sato created an oversized Japanese streetscape within the restaurant, blurring the boundary between the interior and exterior, ground and sky. The company which owns En runs many popular *izakaya* (Japanese pub) restaurants under the same name. The huge success of the flagship restaurant in Shiodome has led to a New York branch—also designed by Sato—scheduled to open in autumn 2004. Using the entrance, pond and gardens as linking intervals, Sato arranged the dining rooms, service stations and passageways such that they formed a frame around the kitchen, the core of any restaurant design. At the entrance, the restaurant's name is handwritten on a plaque fashioned from recycled ship's timber and the glass doors are adorned with black ceramic handles beautifully decorated with bamboo motifs.

6

A complex intertwining of blank spaces, slight gaps, adjoining rooms—details that are associated with traditional Japanese architecture—intrigues the curious diner. Sato purposely designed a chaotic maze to make it difficult to visually estimate the grand size of the restaurant. *Ranma*—the decorative open screens above sliding doors—from a demolished traditional house greet customers as they enter the dining rooms furnished with communal tables shared by different groups of diners, (previous pages). At left is a traditional private dining room located off the entrance hall, finished with a latticework screen and an earthen wall. The connected private dining rooms (right) surrounded by an *engawa* (traditional veranda) are separated by sliding doors fashioned with hand-crafted paper.

Other than the private dining rooms, the restaurant houses a larger dining area that has been furbished with six tables (below). This section has a more modern design, and is separated from the corridor by a striking screen of shaved tempered glass bars. The large pendants suspended above the tables are designed to emit light from the top and bottom to illuminate the bamboo ceiling above and tables below. The *engawa* around a pair of private dining rooms juts out at an angle over a sunken pond located at the end of the central hallway. Counter seats surrounding the busy open-plan kitchen are located behind the sake bar, which displays different varieties of sake.

Yaoya
Japanese Restaurant

2-16-17 Honcho, Kichijoji
Musashino-shi, Tokyo

88 m²

September 1999

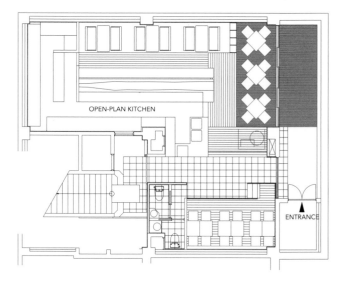

OPEN-PLAN KITCHEN

ENTRANCE

Hoping to capture the Japanese youth market, the owners of Yaoya renovated an established *yakitori* restaurant in a modern style. The restaurant was also renamed "Yaoya," which means "vegetable house" to reflect its revamped menu. Sato's design focuses on highlighting the contrast in materials, such as the gleaming stainless steel of the kitchen equipment with blonde *tamo* wood (Japanese ash). The designer employed various floor levels to create divisions without confining space in the small site. The entrance of black-plate steel and *tamo* wood (below) matches the interior.

A functioning antique well pump (previous pages) is an example of Sato's signature recycling of materials, incorporated into a contemporary design. Recessed lighting accentuates transitional levels between the *tamo* floor and bamboo-finished floor-seating area. The partitioning black-plate steel shelf in the foreground is adorned with vessels used to serve sake. The square *tamo* tables may be readily joined and separated to accommodate any number of customers —a clever way to maximize seating in commercial spaces with high rents, and a reason why many restaurant owners opt for floor seating. The raised, stage-like floor seating area (left and above), a detail often seen in Sato's restaurant designs, is backed by a traditional hand-plastered earthen wall and alcove fitted with recessed lighting.

United Arrows
Boutique

3-28-1 Jingumae
Shibuya-ku, Tokyo

979 m²

September 2003

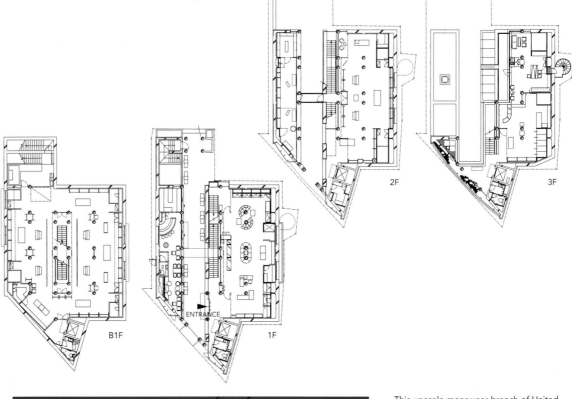

2F

3F

B1F

ENTRANCE

1F

This upscale menswear branch of United Arrows is located in a pair of buildings designed by architect Ricardo Bofil. When the company decided to renovate the shop, Sato was commissioned as designer for the project. The "East Meets West" concept gave Sato a way to incorporate elements of his design ideas into the existing architecture. The installation of the traditional *chochin* (paper lanterns) in the storefront display windows is an example of how Sato achieved this. Stately columns and a central passage intersecting the two narrow buildings (right) are signatures of Bofil's design, which borrows from period architecture.

6

This successful retail brand is well known for a discerning eye in selecting merchandise from different international and domestic collections. On the left, massive columns, emphasized with mirrored ceilings and basal fixtures, illustrate Sato's clever incorporation of new design elements. The second floor (below) houses a collection of imported tailored wear. The floor is of walnut and Indian sandstone. The dramatic *shoji* grid wall is a composition of brass-plated steel pipes and sandblasted glass, another one of the several Japanese elements Sato has introduced with his design concept.

The third floor devoted to custom tailoring and formal wear, is designed to create a salon-like atmosphere of exclusivity. The client's collection of vintage photography seen at left adorns the den-like fitting room. Behind the walnut doors are wardrobes of formal wear (below) that slide into view on grooved tracks set into the carpeted floor. The screens above the doors are finished in traditional Japanese gold leaf and adorned with vintage hats and canes to add to the ambience. On this floor, Sato also designed a tiny tea ceremony room (not shown) for VIP customers. A champagne bar (right) to refresh customers after their shopping spree is located on the ground floor, across the passageway intersecting the two buildings. The old-time atmosphere is accentuated by the flared cornice and an acrylic '60s pendant imported from England.

Pipes of the repeated brass and glass grid walls—seen at left—flanking the basement stairs seamlessly extend into hanger pipes. The basement floor displays a selection of imported sportswear and track shoes and is paved with Indian sandstone. The dress-shoe section (below) is on the narrow upper floor of the secondary building, and showcases the shop's unique collection on built-in shelves lined with leather. The sloped ceiling in walnut veneer creates an intimate environment reminiscent of a cozy attic.

Takao Katsuta recently set up his own studio, Line, having become independent from a design studio/metal furniture workshop called Exit Metal Work Supply, which he co-founded with four colleagues in 1996, in an old house equipped with little else except a secondhand welding machine.

       Katsuta's work can be best described as raw, edgy and hard—qualities which he felt offered a creative solution to the limited budgets of his clients, many of whom were similarly young and upcoming in their respective fields. Together, designer and client scoured old sites in search of weathered textures or some architectural elements that could be integrated into one of their shop designs. Over the years, some of Katsuta's clients, such as Number (N)ine and Frapbois, have now become icons of Japan's youth culture. These clients have commissioned Katsuta to design a number of highly visible projects within and outside of Japan—including a shop in New York.

Craftsmanship skills, culled from years working in a furniture workshop, allow for an attention to detail, and the use of unadorned materials adds touches of elegance and warmth to his designs. Calculated crudeness and untidiness are other signature elements of Katsuta's designs. His obsessive attention to detail and penchant for overlaying materials may mislead us to imagine the designer as a severely high-strung character but oddly enough, he is, in person, an extremely amicable and mischievous individual. In fact he not only delights his clients with his designs, Katsuta is constantly racking his brains in search of the perfect joke or prank to entertain his clients with, and his sense of humor is apparent in many of his projects.

Katsuta's interest in design was first inspired by a part-time job restoring antique furniture while he was in his teens. "I felt a great joy in being able to transform an object into something to be appreciated and used again." Having also been an apprentice in a metal factory for six months—during which he learned to haul raw materials and weld—his initial, natural inclination was to build his designs in steel. "It was fascinating to see how a sheet of steel can be transformed into a three-dimensional object, a design on paper becoming a physical reality," he says. Now he chooses materials based on what each project requires.

Having begun his career designing furniture, Katsuta says that he makes an effort to design retail spaces with the same detailed attention given to designing a chair. "At the initial stages of design, I walk through the visualized design, beginning at the entrance, imagining what a visitor may feel. I try to eliminate visually unattractive or non-functional details before finalizing the design, in order to prevent it from becoming superficial. My ultimate goal is to achieve a space which echoes its own silence by overlaying materials, form and light." In reply to what he wishes for at the moment, Katsuta says he hopes for free time—to design the perfect chair and to travel.

Takao **KATSUTA**

Number (N)ine
Boutique

2-16-6 Ebisu
Shibuya-ku, Tokyo

195 m²

May 2003

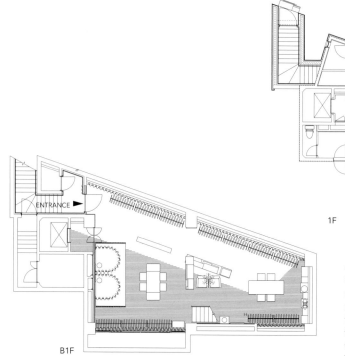

1F

B1F

An antique iron door leading through a brick archway brings you to the underground world of Number (N)ine's eclectic menswear shop. The shop is far removed from the busy street activity in the newly fashionable Ebisu district. Katsuta's design was modeled after charismatic designer Takahiro Miyashita's residence, filled with antiques and peculiar relics collected during his travels. So successful is the designer in realizing his design ideas that customers can almost feel the musty air, like the air in an old secondhand shop, permeating the boutique. An antique baker's rack (below) displays knitwear in the basement floor.

7

An old steel chandelier (previous pages) from an American supermarket hangs in front of a striking wall made of coarsely stripped layers of waterproofing material and adhesive smudged with black paint. Stacks of old books and recycled wooden slabs make a unique display table. On the ground floor, an installation of disposed televisions sets (left) features the latest runway collection in sepia-toned images. Katsuta's obsessive attention to detail and his penchant for overlaying materials is seen in the glass pendants, which have been cracked with a hammer to create unique shapes, and the luxurious French velvet draping the staircase adorned with balustrades (left and below) disassembled from an antique iron shelf found in New York. The wall and floor of the room have been finished with three coats of paint to create a distressed texture, as seen at right. An antique tray placed on the pedestal of a sewing machine functions as a display case for accessories. Shown on the right is the cashier's desk, an assemblage of recycled wood, books and zinc tiles. A vintage wine rack serving as a shoe tree is placed next to the fitting area where the silvering of the mirror framed in zinc tiles has been treated to create an antiquated look.

A dark journey down the stairs from the street entrance to the basement level heightens the sensation of entering an underground world (above). An antique door and fixtures (opposite) adorn the doorway at the bottom of the stairwell, painstakingly fabricated from recycled bricks that were sliced, hammered and smudged with mortar so as to create an aged texture. Numerous speakers have been installed at the back of the shop, an expression of the fashion designer's love of music—the label is named after the Beatles' song "Revolution Number Nine." An exit door leading to the street, seen on the left, is located on the ground floor.

NS
Boutique

1-41 Kaiunbashi-dori
Morioka, Iwate Prefecture

68 m²

May 2001

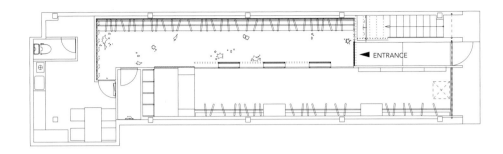

This shop, located in the northern city of Morioka, houses the street fashion label Number (N)ine and the tailored label Soph. Both labels were created by Takahiro Miyashita. Katsuta divided the narrow floor space into two, creating individual areas for the two collections. He designed two contrasting images within the boutique using the concept of opposing magnetic poles repelling and attracting each other to form the coherent whole of a magnetic field. The two spaces are demarcated by sliding glass panels (below). A startling bullet-shattered panel (right) was made by tapping film-laminated glass with a fine-point hammer, then encasing the glass between two sheets of glass. The other panel was mirror-finished and installed with glass shelving.

7

The wall in the Soph section is made of bamboo flooring that has been integrated into the ceiling in a continuous curved line. Linear lighting recessed into the flooring emphasizes the depth of the narrow space. The wall-to-ceiling design is repeated in black-plate skid-proof steel in the Number (N)ine section (below). This design, when viewed as a whole, gives the shop's interior a tunnel-like appearance. The bare concrete floor of the Number (N)ine shop is splattered with tar, echoing the rough-and-ready image of street fashion. As the shop's entrance is a significant distance from the street, Katsuta laminated its automatic door with cherry-red film to call attention to the shop.

World Style
Boutique

1F Toho Bldg
2-7-2 Dogenzaka
Shibuya-ku, Tokyo

22 m²

September 2002

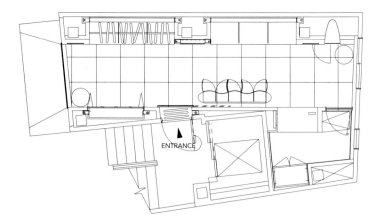

ENTRANCE

World Style has a "hot" reputation among
fashionistas for their fabulous selection of
merchandise from various internationally
acclaimed brands. The owners asked for a
crisp, clean design for this tiny shop, which
is located on the second floor in the thriving
shopping district of Shibuya. To meet their
request, Katsuta created a stark white, tunnel-like space accented by fluorescent green
and reflective finishes. The tunnel concept
is reflected in a curved steel window facade
(right) with an illuminated laser-cut logo. All
compartments in the boutique are recessed
into the wall, maintaining the linear form of
the tunnel. The floor is made of Corian.

7

《 WORLD STYLE 》

Underpass × privateroom

Cylindrical steel cases (left) are fitted with downlights to highlight the displayed wares. Lines of LED lamps installed behind a black tinted glass screen have been digitally programmed to flash in three alternating cycles, to create moving lights similar to those in the opening scene of the film *Matrix*—linear lines, numerical symbols and alphabetical letters repeatedly flash the shop's name. The showcase (above) has been fitted with mirror-finished stainless metal and curved, green tinted glass to complete the cool, polished look.

Nano Universe
Boutique

1-12-17 Jinnan
Shibuya-ku, Tokyo

149 m²

April 1999

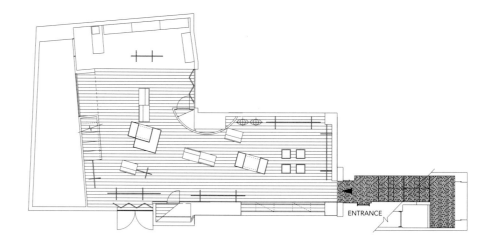

This cutting-edge menswear shop is housed in a combination of spaces that shows a typical example of the architectural oddities in Tokyo. The shop itself is located in the basement of Shibuya Marui, the omnipresent icon of youth fashion culture, while the staircase leading to the entrance is located in an adjacent building. The shop's entrance (right) is located at the bottom of a staircase and was created by literally knocking a hole through the walls of two buildings. Zinc floor plates and a collage made of recycled wood, plates of untreated steel as well as generic exterior lighting fixtures embellish the bare staircase. The floor of the interior is created from wood recycled from a chicken coop.

7

The jagged edge of the entrance (left) has been left intact, recalling the shop's odd history. Katsuta stripped the rooms bare, blatantly exposing their structure. He then installed his signature steel fixtures which were designed in different shapes. The illuminated display table is a composition of four cubes of steel and sandblasted glass. The display staircase in the foreground on the right makes a satirical statement—in contrast to the newly installed staircase at the entrance, this staircase leads nowhere.

Frapbois
Boutique

154 Takoya-cho Higashi-iru
Fuya-cho Takoyakushi-dori
Nakagyo-ku, Kyoto

118 m²

March 2003

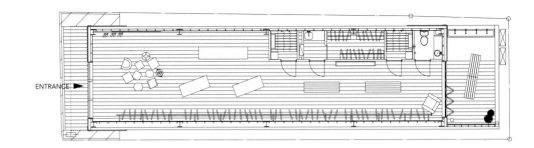

ENTRANCE ▶

This whimsical fashion boutique is located in a long and narrow building wedged between two larger buildings in a quiet Kyoto neighborhood. The designer Eri Utsugi named the label after her favorite toy hammer—Frapbois means "to hit wood" in French. Katsuta was given a tight budget to design the shop's exterior as well as its interior. He created a factory-like space —shown on the right—complete with industrial lamps. The lamps light up the general floor area while hanging spotlights highlight the merchandise. Fabricated in sleek, mirror-finish stainless steel, the cashier's desktop, display tables and the hanger pipes strike a contrast with the recycled wood.

7

Classic doors of the fitting rooms and stock space, seen at left, are fitted into a wall that resembles part of a theater set. An antique armchair, a Persian rug and a 1950s floor lamp designed by Serge Muille add some semblance of a living room atmosphere to an otherwise austere factory environment. Located at the back of the shop is a terrace with a witty installation of a tiled sink (left), reminiscent of those in Japanese primary schools, fitted with only a single functioning faucet. The bench in the foreground (above) provides seating space on sunny days.

A clever display surrounds the armchair (left), inviting the customer to try on some shoes as though she were slipping into them in her own home. In place of his signature custom-designed furnishings, Katsuta dispersed a playful variety of antique chairs, using them as display fixtures, so as to create the visual image of a home strewn with clothing and accessories (right). The parade of chairs is reflected in the mirror, which looks like it is leaning against the wall nonchalantly—this effect was achieved by installing the mirror at a slight angle. Painted surfaces throughout the shop were purposely given a sloppy finish, a detail that fully resonates with the relaxed attitude of Frapbois's creations.

CHRONOLOGY

Akihito FUMITA

Born in Osaka, Fumita graduated from the Osaka University of Arts in 1984. He was employed by Ric Design the same year and served as member of staff until 1995, when he established his own studio. In 1999, Fumita moved his studio from Osaka to Tokyo. His numerous accomplishments include winning the prestigious JCD Design Award Grand Prix in 2002 for the Nissan Gallery Ginza and Nissan Gallery Headquarters projects. He is currently working on his first residential project and preparing a product design proposal for an internationally renowned furniture manufacturer.

BOUTIQUES & SHOPS

 1996

INHALE+EXHALE
2F Kobe Fashion Mart Avenue
6-9 Koyo-cho
Higashinada-ku, Kobe

ERMINE
4F OCAT
1-41-1 Minato-machi
Naniwa-ku, Osaka

WASHINGTON STUDIO
5F Odakyu Station Square Mylord
3-8-1 Sagami-ono
Sagamihara, Kanagawa Prefecture

 1997

INHALE+EXHALE
97-1 Iwagakakiuchi-cho
Kamigamo
Kita-ku, Kyoto

FREE'S SHOP
B2F Namba City
5-1-60 Namba
Chuo-ku, Osaka

TRE PINI
2F Plenty
5-2-3 Kojidai
Nishi-ku, Kobe

ETE
Crysta Nagahori Basement Arcade
2 Minami-senba
Chuo-ku, Osaka

 1998

INHALE+EXHALE (below)
4F Shinkobe Oriental Hotel
1 Kitano-cho
Chuo-ku, Kobe

Fumita fabricated a large inner shell in oriented strand board (OSB), interspersed with unique lighting fixtures and furniture for this branch of the discount suit retailer.

POCKET
1-5 Chuo-cho
Toyooka, Hyogo Prefecture

CHUBBY GANG
6F Parco West Annex
3-29-1 Sakae
Naka-ku, Nagoya

HALF NOTE
4F Hep Five
3-1 Kakuda-cho
Kita-ku, Osaka

 1999

TAKEO KIKUCHI SCULPTURE
4F Shibuya Seibu Department Store
B-Annex
21-1 Udagawa-cho
Shibuya-ku ,Tokyo

TAKEO KIKUCHI SCULPTURE
8F JR Takashimaya Department Store
1-1-4 Mei-eki
Nakamura-ku, Nagoya

THE SUPER SUITS STORE
2F Toho Twin Tower Bldg
1-5-2 Yuraku-cho
Chiyoda-ku, Tokyo

TIC TAC
1F Shibuya Parco Part-3
15-1 Udagawa-cho
Shibuya-ku, Tokyo

ETE
B1F Namba City
5-1-60 Namba
Chuo-ku, Osaka

 2000

TAKEO KIKUCHI SCULPTURE
5F Hankyu Department Store
8-7 Kakuda-cho
Kita-ku, Osaka

TAKEO KIKUCHI DASH
4F Takashimaya Department Store
52 Shin-cho Kawaramachi Nish-iiru
Shijo-dori
Shimogyo-ku, Kyoto

TAKEO KIKUCHI DASH
5F Iwataya Z-Side
2-11-1 Tenjin
Chuo-ku, Fukuoka

TAKEO KIKUCHI DASH
7F Sogo Department Store
8-1-8 Onoedori
Chuo-ku, Kobe

THE SUPER SUITS STORE
Crost Osaka Station
3-1-1 Umeda
Kita-ku, Osaka

M-PREMIER
Diamond Basement Arcade
1 Umeda
Kita-ku, Osaka

ETE
6-11-3 Minami Aoyama
Minato-ku, Tokyo

 2001

M-PREMIER
1F Tennoji Mio
10-39 Hidenin-cho
Tennoji-ku, Osaka

M-PREMIER
2F Hankyu Department Store
2-5-1 Yuraku-cho
Chiyoda-ku, Tokyo

M-PREMIER
2F Mitsukoshi Department Store
4-6-16 Ginza
Chuo-ku, Tokyo

M-PREMIER
Shinsaibashi Shopping Arcade
1-6-1 Shinsaibashi
Chuo-ku, Osaka

SUITS & SUITS
Senso-jii Nitenmon-mae
2-34-3 Asakusa
Taito-ku, Tokyo

SUITS & SUITS
B2F Kobe Harbor Circus
1-3-3 Higashi-kawasakucho
Chuo-ku, Kobe

 2002

M-PREMIER
2F Isetan Department Store
3-14-1 Shinjuku
Shinjuku-ku, Tokyo

M-PREMIER (below)
B1F Takashimaya Department Store
5-15-5 Namba
Chuo-ku, Osaka

"A maximum in white" was the concept for this boutique designed with acrylic marble light walls similar to the other branch featured in this volume.

M-PREMIER
5F Takashimaya Department Store
1-1-4 Meieki
Nakamura-ku, Nagoya

ROOM IN BLOOM (below)
B1F Takashimaya Department Store
West Annex
5-15-5 Namba
Chuo-ku, Osaka

M'S SELECT
Diamond Station Basement Arcade
1 Umeda
Kita-ku, Osaka

INHALE+EXHALE
2F Tokyu Department Store
2-24-1 Dogenzaka
Shibuya-ku, Tokyo

IXC. COLLECTA
1F Takashimaya Shopping Center
South Annex
3-17-1 Tamagawa
Setagaya-ku, Tokyo

M-PREMIER
2F Kokura Isetan Department Store
3-1-1 Kyomachi, Kokura Kita-Ku
Kita-kyushu, Fukuoka Prefecture

M-PREMIER
2F Tenmaya Department Store
5-22 Ebisu-cho
Naka-ku, Hiroshima

VOICEMAIL
4F Tenmaya Department Store
5-22 Ebisu-cho
Naka-ku, Hiroshima

M-PREMIER
2F Isetan Department Store
3-14-1 Shinjuku
Shinjuku-ku, Tokyo

HAIR SALONS, HEALTH SPAS & COSMETIC DENTAL CLINICS

K-TWO
1+2F Shinsaibashi New Kiyomi Bldg
1-13-5 Nishi-shinsaibashi
Chuo-ku, Osaka

NATURAL BODY
B1F Namba City
5-1-60 Namba
Chuo-ku, Osaka

NATURAL BODY
B1F Zest Oike
498 Shimo Honnojimae-cho
Nakagyo-ku, Kyoto

NATURAL BODY
10F Parco South Annex
3-29-1 Sakae
Naka-ku, Nagoya

K-TWO
B1F Komodo Bldg
1-52 Chayamachi
Kita-ku, Osaka

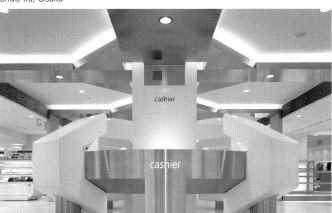

This design commission called for the renovation of a former machine room, which measured 33,000 m², into retail space. The cash desk takes center stage of the spacious layout plan.

VOICEMAIL
2F Yokohama Lumine
2-16-1 Takashima
Nishi-ku, Yokohama

FLASH BE
Santica No 5
1-10-1 Sannomiya
Chuo-ku, Kobe

M-PREMIER
3F Daimaru Department Store
East Annex
1-4-1 Tenjin
Chuo-ku, Fukuoka

M-PREMIER
1F Hankyu Department Store
68 Shin-cho Kawaramachi
Higashi-iru Shijo-dori
Shimogyo-ku, Kyoto

INHALE+EXHALE
1F Yoshikawa Kosan Bldg
5-4-35 Minami-aoyama
Minato-ku, Tokyo

M-PREMIER BLACK
3F Hankyu Department Store
8-7 Kakuda-cho
Kita-ku, Osaka

M,I,D, SHOP
2F Hankyu Department Store
8-7 Kakuda-cho
Kita-ku, Osaka

M,I,D, SHOP
2F Hankyu Department Store
2-5-1 Yuraku-cho
Chiyoda-ku, Tokyo

ETE BEAU
3F Roppongi Hills West Walk
6-10-1 Roppongi
Minato-ku, Tokyo

RESTAURANTS & CAFES

MARINA DE BOURBON
4F Decks Tokyo Beach
1-6-1 Daiba
Minato-ku, Tokyo

CHANTO & CHANTO SUPER LIGHTS
2F Osaka City Dome
3-2-1 Chiyozaki
Nishi-ku, Osaka

CAFE *ASTERISK
B1F Takashimaya Department Store
West Annex
5-15-5 Namba
Chuo-ku, Osaka

K-TWO
2F Namba Nikko Bldg
2-4-2 Nishi-shinsaibashi
Chuo-ku, Osaka

ADD
1+2F Shinsaibashi New Kiyomi Bldg
1-13-5 Nishi-shinsaibashi
Chuo-ku, Osaka

NATURAL BODY
B2F Kobe International House Sol
8-1-6 Goko-dori
Chuo-ku, Kobe

NATURAL BODY
4F Shibuya Parco Part-3
15-1 Udagawa-cho
Shibuya-ku, Tokyo

2000

NATURAL BODY
1F Hotel Hankyu International
19-19 Chayamachi
Kita-ku, Osaka

NATURAL BODY
4F Akasaka Belle Vie
3-1-6 Akasaka
Minato-ku, Tokyo

 2001

NATURAL BODY
3F Mycal Town
8-30-4 Matsugamoto-cho
Ibaraki, Osaka

TOOTH LOVED
7F Marui Department Store
1-3-1 Tsudanuma
Narashino, Chiba Prefecture

 2002

BEAUTY SALON
B1F Takashimaya Department Store
West Annex
5-15-5 Namba
Chuo-ku, Osaka

THINK TOOTH
Whity Umeda East Mall
4-3 Umeda Basement Arcade
Komatsubara-cho
Kita-ku, Osaka

 2003

JINGUMAE ORTHODONITICS
801 Trinity Bldg
3-23-3 Jingumae
Shibuya-ku, Tokyo

 2004

NAIL STATION
1F Tama Plaza Tokyu
Shopping Center
1-7 Utsukushigaoka
Aoba-ku, Yokohama

OFFICES, SHOWROOMS & TRADE SHOWS

 1998

MID SHOWROOM
1F Hatto Bldg
4-3-3 Bingo-machi
Chuo-ku, Osaka

 1999

DAIKO BOOTH —
1999 LIGHTING FAIR (below)
Tokyo Big Sight
3-21-1 Ariake
Koto-ku, Tokyo

Fireproof nylon mesh originally utilized for temporary enclosures of construction sites was used for these impressive shades in the lighting manufacturer's booth window.

 2001

NISSAN GALLERY HEADQUARTERS
1F Nissan Headquarter Office Bldg
6-17-1 Ginza
Chuo-ku, Tokyo

NISSAN BOOTH —
35TH TOKYO MOTOR SHOW
Makuhari Messe
2-1 Nakase
Mihama-ku, Chiba

LITTLE ANDERSEN OFFICE
AM Bldg
5-42-14 Jingumae
Shibuya-ku, Tokyo

 2002

NISSAN GALLERY NAGOYA
Sakae Basement Arcade
3-4-6 Sakae
Naka-ku, Nagoya

NISSAN GALLERY FUKUOKA
4F IMS Bldg
1-7-11 Tenjin
Chuo-ku, Fukuoka

NISSAN BOOTH —
36TH TOKYO MOTOR SHOW
Makuhari Messe
2-1 Nakase
Mihama-ku, Chiba

NISSAN DIESEL BOOTH —
36TH TOKYO MOTOR SHOW
Makuhari Messe
2-1 Nakase
Mihama-ku, Chiba

 2003

ARAKAWA GRIP BOOTH —
2003 JAPAN SHOP
Big Sight
3-21-1 Ariake
Koto-ku, Tokyo

NISSAN BOOTH —
37TH TOKYO MOTOR SHOW
Makuhari Messe
2-1 Nakase
Mihama-ku, Chiba

L.A. LOGISTICS
13-4 Wakamatsu-cho
Chigasaki, Kanagawa Prefecture

EXHIBITIONS

 1999

"NEXT STANDARD—
SIX INTERIOR DESIGNERS"
Muse Gallery
Minami-horie, Osaka

 2001

"NEW FURNITURE AND
LIGHTING DESIGN" —
TOKYO DESIGNERS BLOCK 2001
Omni Q Gallery
Aoyama, Tokyo

 2003

"NEW FURNITURE AND
LIGHTING DESIGN" —
TOKYO DESIGNERS BLOCK 2003
Gallery Kitamura
Aoyama, Tokyo

Yukio HASHIMOTO

Hashimoto was born in Aichi Prefecture. In 1986, he graduated from the Aichi Prefectural University of Fine Arts and Music after which he joined the staff of Super Potato before setting up his own studio in 1997. He is currently lecturing at the Women's College of Fine Arts and Aichi Prefectural University of Fine Arts and Music. Hashimoto has been the recipient of numerous awards, among which are the JCD Encouragement Award in 1998 and 1999, and the JCD Second Award in 2000. He is now also involved in residential projects as well as product design.

RESTAURANTS & BARS

 1996

PLAT
B1F Saeki-Bldg
1-18-15 Shinbashi
Minato-ku, Tokyo

SHAMO-SHO
2-13-15 Nishi-azabu
Minato-ku, Tokyo

 1997

LA BETTOLA da OCHIAI
1-21-2 Ginza
Chuo-ku, Tokyo

TARUSAKU
1-43-4 Tougane-cho
Katsushika-ku, Tokyo

UOGASHI MEICHA CHANOMI CLUB
2-11-12 Tsukiji
Chuo-ku, Tokyo

MITSUI
B1F Villa Acolde
2-51-1 Ikebukuro
Toshima-ku, Tokyo

1998

TASTE VIN AOYAMA
B1F Kemmy Court
6-15-6 Minami-aoyama
Minato-ku, Tokyo

GRANATA
B1F T.B.S Kaikan
5-3-3 Akasaka
Minato-ku, Tokyo

ZASSOYA
B1F Belte Plaza
4-1-15 Minami-aoyama
Minato-ku, Tokyo

DAIDAIYA SHINJUKU
3F Shinjuku Nowa Bldg
3-37-12 Shinjuku
Shinjuku-ku, Tokyo

1999

TOPS & GRANATA
B1F Sanwa Bldg
4-6-1 Ginza
Chuo-ku, Tokyo

AZUMIYA
B2F Dim Ginza Bldg
6-7-18 Ginza
Chuo-ku, Tokyo

TSURUMAE
1F Sutera Kijima
3-24-4 Koenji-minami
Suginami-ku, Tokyo

KURA
3-1-13 Koenji-kita
Suginami-ku, Tokyo

CAFE SUZUKI
101 Rockhills Honatsugi-ekimae
3-5-6 Nakamachi
Atsugi, Kanagawa Prefecture

2000

BANNOYAKU (below)
1F Fujikura Heights
1-3-1 Ebisu-nishi
Shibuya-ku, Tokyo

This Korean restaurant, whose name means "panacea," was designed with a series of glass screens intricately printed with traditional Korean lotus and arabesque tile motifs

G ROUGE
B1F Tsukiji Nishiyama Bldg
1-10-7 Tsukiji
Chuo-ku, Tokyo

DAIDAIYA GINZA
2F Ginza 9 Bldg No1
8-5 Nishi-ginza
Chuo-ku, Tokyo

TAKADAYA
1F Ueno Suzumoto Bldg
2-7-12 Ueno
Taito-ku, Tokyo

DANCHU
2F Ueno Suzumoto Bldg
2-7-12 Ueno
Taito-ku, Tokyo

GIURARE
Unimat Bit Creek House
5-17-22 Jingumae
Shibuya-ku, Tokyo

AZABU KOGAICHO MANPUKU
2F Nishi-azabu Chisei Bldg
4-7-10 Nishi-azabu
Minato-ku, Tokyo

DAIDAIYA AKASAKA
9F Bellvie Akasaka
3-1-6 Akasaka
Minato-ku, Tokyo

GINZA KAMONKA
B1F Ginza First Bldg
1-10-6 Ginza
Chuo-ku, Tokyo

TORAJI
4F 6-3-11 Ginza
Chuo-ku, Tokyo

LA SO
Roppongi Village
3-12-41 Moto-azabu
Minato-ku, Tokyo

CLUB HIKA
70-3 Motoyoshi-cho Gion Shinbashi
Higashiyama-ku, Kyoto

2001

SEN-NINDOSHIN
2F 2-2-4 Surugadai Kanda
Chiyoda-ku, Tokyo

RYUMON
1F Shinbashi 2nd Bldg
2-3-7 Shinbashi
Minato-ku, Tokyo

REGALO
B1F 1-4-7 Nishi-shinjuku
Shinjuku-ku, Tokyo

SHASHUISEN (below)
6F Isetan Kaikan
3-15-17 Shinjuku
Shinjuku-ku, Tokyo

TEUCHI SOBA DAIAN
2F Daian Bldg
3-36-6 Shinjuku
Shinjuku-ku, Tokyo

AZIE
1F Grand Formosa Regent Taipei
41 Chung Shan N Rd, Section 2
Taipei, Taiwan

JYABUYA
1F Daiichi Kyoei Bldg
1-7-3 Ebisu
Shibuya-ku, Tokyo

2002

TSUKI NO SHIZUKU
6F Humax Pavilion Bldg
1-21-2 Minami-ikebukuro
Toshima-ku, Tokyo

AJIKAGURA HONATSUGI
2F Odakyu Atsugi Hotel
1-1 Izumi-cho
Atsugi, Kanagawa Prefecture

UDON DINING KOMUGI
2F Erika Bldg
1-21-5 Asakusa
Taito-ku, Tokyo

DAIDAIYA YOKOHAMA QUEEN'S SQUARE
4F Queen's Square Yokohama at 2nd
2-3-8 Minato-mirai
Nishi-ku, Yokohama

The interior of this striking contemporary Japanese restaurant shows a collaboration between Hashimoto and artist Saika, whose calligraphy works are painted with crushed shell powder.

TORAJI CHU-HA-CHU-DONG
6F Marunouchi Bldg
2-4-1 Marunouchi
Chiyoda-ku, Tokyo

TERRACE VERVERGE
3-jo 10-chome Miyanomori
Chuo-ku, Sapporo

ROBIN'S
3F Grand Formosa Regent Taipei
41 Chung Shan N Rd, Section 2
Taipei, Taiwan

SHIGOIN
B1F Glass Square
4-20-4 Ebisu
Shibuya-ku, Tokyo

JINYA
B1F Ahika Bldg 2
1-48 Omiyanaka-cho
Saitama, Saitama Prefecture

LONG FANG
1F Hanayagi Bldg
2-15-10 Akasaka
Minato-ku, Tokyo

CHASHUYA
Hagiwara Bldg
2-6-1 Monzen-nakacho
Koto-ku, Tokyo

 2003

CUISINE!
2F Nihonbashi Plaza Bldg
2-3-4 Nihonbashi
Chuo-ku, Tokyo

SUSHI TOSHIKIAN
1F AO Bldg
3-28-7 Shibuya
Shibuya-ku, Tokyo

MAIMON
1F Fujimizaka Place
3-17-29 Nishi-azabu
Minato-ku, Tokyo

CHASHUYA
1F Daimon Miami Bldg
2-4-1 Shiba-daimon
Minato-ku, Tokyo

KANYA HOUSE OF KOREA (below)
5-8-11 Hiroo
Shibuya-ku, Tokyo

The colorful palette of this modernized Korean restaurant was based on the vivid colors of the *chima jeogori* (traditional Korean costume).

UMEKO NO IE
Emachu Sakura Bldg
2-3-18 Nihonbashi
Chuo-ku, Tokyo

BALLROOM
3F Grand Formosa Regent Taipei
41 Chung Shan N Rd, Section 2
Taipei, Taiwan

OGON NO SHITA
3F Ginza Seiwa Bldg
1-5-6 Shinbashi
Minato-ku, Tokyo

BOUTIQUES & SHOPS

 1996

JOLY NANA
Shinjuku My City
3-38-1 Shinjuku
Shinjuku-ku, Tokyo

IZYM
4F Marui Men's Annex
3-1-20 Shinjuku
Shinjuku-ku, Tokyo

 1999

SAB STREET
La Cerena
1-1-43 Abeno
Abeno-ku, Osaka

BASSETTE WALKER
5F Shibuya Parco Part-1
15-1 Udagawa-cho
Shibuya-ku, Tokyo

**UOGASHI MEICHA
TSUKIJI HONTEN**
4-10-1 Tsukiji
Chuo-ku, Tokyo

SUKENO SHOWROOM
2-8-2 Yagumo
Meguro-ku, Tokyo

 2002

BEAMS HOUSE
1F Marunouchi Bldg
2-4-1 Marunouchi
Chiyoda-ku, Tokyo

 2003

BEAMS
3F Shinsaibashi AXY
2-8-2 Shinsaibashi-suji
Chuo-ku, Osaka

BEAUTY SALONS & CLINICS

 2001

TAKANO YURI BEAUTY SPA (below)
8F Shinjuku Lumine
1-1-5 Nishi-shinjuku
Shinjuku-ku, Tokyo

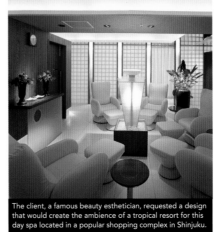

The client, a famous beauty esthetician, requested a design that would create the ambience of a tropical resort for this day spa located in a popular shopping complex in Shinjuku.

 2002

TAKANO YURI BEAUTY SPA
8F Ginza Opaque
3-5-8 Ginza
Chuo-ku, Tokyo

AKAI CLINIC
3+4F KNK Bldg
3-5-17 Kita-aoyama
Minato-ku Tokyo

OFFICES

 1997

CIBA SPECIALTY CHEMICALS K.K.
Takarazuka, Hyogo Prefecture

PROPERTY DESIGN OFFICE
1-19-1 Kanamecho
Toshima-ku, Tokyo

RESIDENCES

 1996

YOSHIDA HOUSE
Nerima-ku, Tokyo

 1997

YOSHII HOUSE
Musashino-shi, Tokyo

 2001

T HOUSE
Setagaya-ku, Tokyo

 2002

H HOUSE
Setagaya-ku, Tokyo

 2003

HM HOUSE
Suginami-ku, Tokyo

TIEN-MOU QIJI CONDOMINIUMS
Taipei, Taiwan

Takao KATSUTA

Born in Shizuoka Prefecture, Katsuta co-founded Exit Metal Work Supply with four colleagues in 1996 before establishing his own studio in 2002. His present commitments include overseeing the architectural and interior design direction for a mammoth project measuring 3,000 m² for the Fukuoka Visionary Arts School, designing showrooms for a renowned motorcycle manufacturer in Asia Pacific, and a boutique in London. He recently set up a company that produces and markets his original furniture designs.

BOUTIQUES & SHOPS

 1998

THE 6TH MAN COMPANY
1F Pine Bldg
17-18 Sarugaku-cho
Shibuya-ku, Tokyo

A.I.P
B1+1F Garden Terrace
6-1-4 Jingumae
Shibuya-ku, Tokyo

 1999

T6M
13-6 Daikanyama-cho
Shibuya-ku, Tokyo

A.I.P
3F Sapporo Parco
Minami 1-jo Nishi 3-chome
Chuo-ku, Sapporo

 2000

EBONY & IVORY (below)
2-12-18 Yamamoto-dori
Chuo-ku, Kobe

The massive fixture, positioned in the center of the boutique, is designed in the image of the crucifix, with a series of crosses and red blood-like paint stains.

CRAMP
1F Ono Bldg
3-22-18 Sakae
Naka-ku, Nagoya

NUMBER (N)INE
2-16-6 Ebisu
Shibuya-ku, Tokyo

A.I.P
Omiya Marui
2-3 Sakuragi-cho
Omiya-ku, Saitama

A.I.P
Shizuoka Marui
6-10 Miyuki-cho
Shizuoka, Shizuoka Prefecture

 2001

FRAPBOIS
1-20-4 Aobadai
Meguro-ku, Tokyo

MILLION AIR
6-18-2 Jingumae
Shibuya-ku, Tokyo

MANO
1F Tokyo Bay Lalaport Part-1
2-1-1 Hama-cho
Funabashi, Chiba Prefecture

MANO
1F Sunshine City Alpa
3-1 Higashi-ikebukuro
Toshima-ku, Tokyo

MANO
3F Aqua City
1-7-1 Daiba
Minato-ku, Tokyo

NULV
1F Yokohama Sky Bldg
2-19-12 Takashima
Nishi-ku, Yokohama

FRAPBOIS
1F Zaza City Hamamatsu
100-1 Hamamatsu
Kajimachi, Shizuoka Prefecture

 2002

NANO UNIVERSE
1+2F Unimat Crystal Point
1-19-14 Jinnan
Shibuya-ku, Tokyo

FRAPBOIS
2-1-9 Ryogae-cho
Shizuoka, Shizuoka Prefecture

FRAPBOIS
3F Sapporo Parco
Minami 1-jo Nishi 3-chome
Chuo-ku, Sapporo

MANO
3F Kichijoji Parco
1-5-1 Kichijoji Hon-cho
Musashino-shi, Tokyo

A.I.P
5F Shibuya Parco Part-1
15-1 Udagawa-cho
Shibuya-ku, Tokyo

FRAPBOIS
2F Hakata Izutsuya
1-1 Hakata-eki Chuo-gai
Hakata-ku, Fukuoka

FRAPBOIS
3F Nagoya Parco West Annex
3-29-1 Sakae
Naka-ku, Nagoya

A.I.P
Sapporo Parco
Minami 1-jo Nishi 3-chome
Chuo-ku, Sapporo

A.I.P
4F Ikebukuro Parco
1-28-2 Minami-ikebukuro
Toshima-ku, Tokyo

 2003

FRAPBOIS
1F Revolution Bldg
2-8-26 Chuo
Aoba-ku, Sendai

FRAPBOIS
1-13-18 Daimyo
Chuo-ku, Fukuoka

NANO UNIVERSE
Yokohama Lumine
2-16-1 Takashima
Nishi-ku, Yokohama

LEVI'S
2F Daikanyama Juban Bldg
10-1 Daikanyama-cho
Shibuya-ku, Tokyo

NUMBER (N)INE (below)
431 Washington St
New York, New York 10013

Katsuta and staff stacked the antique books and recycled wood for the cash desk in the old New York site, the inspiration for the Ebisu branch design featured in this volume.

RUPERT
6F Meitetsu Seven
1-2-1 Mei-eki
Nakamura-ku, Nagoya

DGRACE
5F Atre Ebisu
1-5-5 Ebisu-minami
Shibuya-ku, Tokyo

ET VOUS
2F Aoyama Bell Commons
2-14-6 Kita-aoyama
Minato-ku, Tokyo

RUPERT
Namba Parks
2-8-110 Namba-naka
Naniwa-ku, Osaka

EV BY ET VOUS
Namba Parks
2-8-110 Namba-naka
Naniwa-ku, Osaka

FRAPBOIS
3F Shibuya Parco Part-1
15-1 Udagawa-cho
Shibuya-ku, Tokyo

MANO
Namba Parks
2-8-110 Namba-naka
Naniwa-ku, Osaka

LANCHIKI CENTRAAAAAL AOYAMA
5-45-12 Jingumae
Shibuya-ku, Tokyo

DGRACE
Machida Marui
6-1-6 Hara-machida
Machida-shi, Tokyo

ART & SCIENCE
100 Daikanyama Ivy
9-3 Daikanyama-cho
Shibuya-ku, Tokyo

MANO
5F Atre Ebisu
1-5-5 Ebisu-minami
Shibuya-ku, Tokyo

FRAPBOIS (below)
1F 2-36-2 Kitazawa
Setagaya-ku, Tokyo

One wall of this shop located in the center of Tokyo youth culture, Shimokitazawa, was entirely mirrored to create a semblance of infinite depth.

BEAUTY : BEAST
1F Fujiya Bldg
1-3-9 Kami-meguro
Meguro-ku, Tokyo

MANO
2F JR Tower Stellar Place
Kita 5-jo Nishi 2-chome 5
Chuo-ku, Sapporo

CORWICH CRAFT
2F Daikanyama Address Dix-Sept
17-6 Daikanyama-cho
Shibuya-ku, Tokyo

FRAPBOIS
A Annex
19-5 Sarugaku-cho
Shibuya-ku, Tokyo

DGRACE
Tachikawa Grandio
3-2-1 Shibasaki-cho
Tachikawa-shi, Tokyo

EV BY ET VOUS
2F Yokohama Marui City
2-19-12 Takashima
Nishi-ku, Yokohama

ET VOUS
5F Nagoya Takashimaya
1-1-4 Mei-eki
Nakamura-ku, Nagoya

RESTRICTION
Yokohama Joinus
1-5-30 Minami-saiwai
Nishi-ku, Yokohama

RESTAURANTS & BARS

 2002

MARBLE
2-14-2 Koenji-minami
Suginami-ku, Tokyo

WASABI BISTRO OF HONOLULU
2F La Cittadella
4-1 Ogawa-cho
Kawasaki, Kanagawa Prefecture

NOMAD
2-19-5 Nezu
Bunkyo-ku, Tokyo

YOU XIAN
IF Glassarea
5-4-41 Minami-aoyama
Minato-ku, Tokyo

 2003

DIM SUM CAFE 'LIU
3-8-1 Sagami-ono
Sagamihara, Kanagawa Prefecture

NEXUS CHARBROIL-GRILL
6-15-102 Minami-fujisawa
Fujisawa, Kanagawa Prefecture

HAIR SALONS

 2003

ROCKETS
2F Assembly Ebisu
3-2-2 Ebisu-minami
Shibuya-ku, Tokyo

OFFICES & TRADE SHOWS

 1999

A.I.P HEAD OFFICE
5F 1-22-11 Higashi
Shibuya-ku, Tokyo

 2000

RENOMA EXHIBITION
2-5-1 Kita-aoyama
Minato-ku, Tokyo

 2001

NUMBER (N)INE OFFICE
2-16-6 Ebisu
Shibuya-ku, Tokyo

 2002

GUADELOUPE OFFICE
301 2-7 Sarugaku-cho
Shibuya-ku, Tokyo

ADACHI GAKUEN AOYAMA OFFICE
7F 6-11-1 Minami-aoyama
Minato-ku, Tokyo

NUMBER (N)INE OFFICE
3+5+6F Maruishi Bldg
1-31-9 Ebisu
Shibuya-ku, Tokyo

"EXHIBITION WHITE NUMBER (N)INE" (below)
1F Takemoto Bldg
3-3-21 Minami-aoyama
Minato-ku, Tokyo

An exhibition was held to launch a book featuring the fashion label's original denim fabric—which was also used to upholster the tables, shelving and stools. One hundred stools were sold in a day.

 2003

ROYAL ARTS SHIBUYA OFFICE
30-9 Sakuraoka-machi
Shibuya-ku, Tokyo

NANO UNIVERSE OFFICE
3F 1-19-14 Jinnan
Shibuya-ku, Tokyo

ADACHI GAKUEN HARAJUKU OFFICE
6-10-11 Jingumae
Shibuya-ku, Tokyo

YAMAHA BOOTH — 37TH TOKYO MOTOR SHOW
Makuhari Messe
2-1 Nakase, Mihama-ku
Chiba, Chiba Prefecture

OZOC EXHIBITION
3-5-5 Nishi-azabu
Minato-ku, Tokyo

Tsutomu KUROKAWA

From 1987 to 1992, Nagoya-born Kurokawa worked at the design firm Super Potato. His stint with the company ended when he and his colleague Masamichi Katayama decided to set up H.Design Associates. They held their first furniture exhibition, entitled "H.Design—Furnitures BALANCE" in 1997, which marked the beginning of the series of furniture exhibitions held in Tokyo, Milan and Paris. Kurokawa established Out Design in 2000, after the two designers parted ways to pursue individual careers.

BOUTIQUES & SHOPS

 1996

YOICHI NAGASAWA
1F KR House
5-3-17 Jingumae
Shibuya-ku, Tokyo

 1997

NO CONCEPT BUT GOOD SENSE
2F Cosmo Bldg
5-45-2 Jingumae
Shibuya-ku, Tokyo

 1998

PAS DE CALAIS
4F Shibuya Parco
15-1 Udagawa-cho
Shibuya-ku, Tokyo

PAS DE CALAIS
3F Nagoya Parco West Annex
3-29-1 Sakae
Naka-ku, Nagoya

KORS BY MICHAEL KORS
Shinjuku Odakyu Department Store
1-1-3 Nishi-shinjuku
Shinjuku-ku, Tokyo

 1999

NO CONCEPT BUT GOOD SENSE
1F Wellbeing Bldg
1-15-24 Ona
Chuo-ku, Fukuoka

UNDERCOVER MENS
2F Nowhere
2-5-8 Minami-aoyama
Minato-ku, Tokyo

UNDERCOVER MENS
2F Nowhere
4-11-27 Chiyoda-cho
Maebashi, Gunma Prefecture

VIA BUS STOP GARAGE
3F Laforet Harajuku
1-11-6 Jingumae
Shibuya-ku, Tokyo

 2000

NO CONCEPT BUT GOOD SENSE
6-30-3 Jingumae
Shibuya-ku, Tokyo

HOCQUY
1F Address Garden Daikanyama
6-15 Daikanyama-cho
Shibuya-ku, Tokyo

UTH
4-31-5 Jingumae
Shibuya-ku, Tokyo

 2001

ADAM et ROPE
1F Hiroshima Parco
2-1 Shintenchi
Naka-ku, Hiroshima

ADAM et ROPE
1F Sannomiya Opa
8-1-2 Kumoi-dori
Chuo-ku, Kobe

UTH
1F Creare
3-18-1 Sakae
Naka-ku, Nagoya

UTH
1F Kintestu Hoop
1-2-30 Abeno-suji
Abeno-ku, Osaka

 2002

PINCEAU
2F Marunouchi Bldg
2-4-1 Marunouchi
Chiyoda-ku, Tokyo

ADAM et ROPE
1F Fujii Daimaru
605 Teianmaeno-cho Shijo-sagaru
Teramachi-dori
Sakyo-ku Kyoto

ADAM et ROPE (below)
1F Sapporo Parco
Minami 1-jo Nishi 3-chome
Chuo-ku, Sapporo

 2003

PAS DE CALAIS
4F Shibuya Parco Part-1
15-1 Udagawa-cho
Shibuya-ku, Tokyo

HOCQUY
3F JR Tower Stellar Place
Kita 5-jo Nishi 2-chome 5
Chuo-ku, Sapporo

HOCQUY
1-3-14 Daimyo
Chuo-ku, Fukuoka

HARE
1-12-4 Minami-horie
Nishi-ku, Osaka

Blatantly defying the trend of unified design, Kurokawa created a composition of diverse materials and fixtures for this branch of the successful brand offering fashion for both sexes.

ADAM et ROPE + PINCEAU
1F Shinsaibashi Opa
1-4-3 Nishi-shinsaibashi
Chuo-ku, Osaka

LOWRY'S FARM
1F 1-2-14 Daimyo
Chuo-ku, Fukuoka

GLOBAL WORK
2-3F 1-2-14 Daimyo
Chuo-ku, Fukuoka

PINCEAU
1F Nagoya Parco West Annex
3-29-1 Sakae
Naka-ku, Nagoya

LOWRY'S FARM
1-17-3 Jinnan
Shibuya-ku, Tokyo

LOWRY'S FARM
3F Cial
1-1-1 Nanko
Nishi-ku, Yokohama

RAGE BLUE
6F Tachikawa Lumine
2-1-1 Akebono-cho
Tachikawa-shi, Tokyo

SUBSCRIBE
1-3-14 Daimyo
Chuo-ku, Fukuoka

RESTAURANTS & BARS

1995

CLUB HANAKO
2F Square Bldg
3-10-3 Roppongi
Minato-ku, Tokyo

2002

KOWLOON TENSHIN (below)
7F Shinjuku My City
3-38-1 Shinjuku
Shinjuku-ku, Tokyo

Lattice motifs, curvatures and circular forms—what Kurokawa considers quintessentially Chinese—were employed as icons in the overall contemporary design for this *dim sum* restaurant.

LUUK CHANG
7F Shinjuku My City
3-38-1 Shinjuku
Shinjuku-ku, Tokyo

OFFICES, SHOWROOMS & TRADE SHOWS

1995

LIGHTING PLANNERS ASSOCIATES
5-28-10 Jingumae
Shibuya-ku, Tokyo

FUJIYA GALLERY
2F Fujiya Bldg
2-6-5 Ginza
Chuo-ku, Tokyo

2002

SUN AD — Meeting room
7F Palace Bldg
1-1-1 Marunouchi
Chiyoda-ku, Tokyo

GALERIE DE POP — Pressroom
5-17-10 Shiroganedai
Minato-ku, Tokyo

2003

"DE BEERS LV EXHIBITION"
2-20-7 Ebisu-minami
Shibuya-ku, Tokyo

PRODUCTS

1992

"303" — Table
Materials: cherry, plywood, chrome-plated steel
Manufacturer: Time & Style (Prestige Japan, Inc)

1996

"902" — Table
Materials: walnut, chrome-plated steel
Manufacturer: Time & Style (Prestige Japan, Inc)

"TP" — TV Monitor with Stand
Materials: chrome-plated steel
Manufacturer: Time & Style (Prestige Japan, Inc)

1997

"MILLE" — Bookshelf
Materials: walnut, polyester mesh, chrome-plated steel
Manufacturer: Time & Style (Prestige Japan, Inc)

"LUSE" — Suspension Lighting
Materials: steel and fluorescent lamps
Manufacturer: Time & Style (Prestige Japan, Inc)

"QUARK" — Carpet
Materials: wool
Manufacturer: Time & Style (Prestige Japan, Inc)

"CUSH" — Cushion with Frame
Materials: fabric, steel
Manufacturer: Time & Style (Prestige Japan, Inc)

1998

"RUKIO" — Audiovisual Cabinet
Materials: wood, polyester mesh, steel
Manufacturer: Time & Style (Prestige Japan, Inc)

"QUIT" — TV Stand
Materials: wood, chrome-plated steel, aluminum
Manufacturer: Time & Style (Prestige Japan, Inc)

"VOTCH" — Armchair and Sofa
Materials: fabric, wood frame
Manufacturer: Time & Style (Prestige Japan, Inc)

"TABLE LARG" — Coffee-Table
Materials: teak, chrome-plated steel
Manufacturer: Aidec Co Ltd

"FLOW" — Lighting Fixture Series
Materials: half-mirrored polycarbonate, steel, wood
Manufacturer: Daiko Electric Co Ltd

"LARG" — Armchair and Sofa
Materials: fabric, chrome-plated steel
Manufacturer: Aidec Co Ltd

2000

"OLBERI" — Table Series
Materials: acrylic resin, wood
Manufacturer: Waazwiz Ltd

"MAPELL" — Chair and Stool
Materials: polycarbonate, fabric
Manufacturer: Waazwiz Ltd

"MAPELL ACRYLIC CHAIR" — Chair
Materials: polycarbonate, acrylic resin
Manufacturer: Waazwiz Ltd

2001

"MA CAFE TABLE" — Table
Materials: polycarbonate, acrylic resin, chrome-plated steel
Manufacturer: Waazwiz Ltd

"MA BOOKSHELF" — Bookshelf
Materials: polycarbonate, acrylic resin
Manufacturer: Waazwiz Ltd

"PAPINA" — Chair
Materials: fabric, chrome-plated steel
Manufacturer: Idee Co Ltd

"KALFA" — Chair
Materials: aluminum, plywood
Manufacturer: Aidec Co Ltd

"QUNTE" — Chair
Materials: acrylic resin
Manufacturer: Waazwiz Ltd

"MATY" — Lighting Fixture (below)
Materials: acrylic resin, LED lamps
Manufacturer: Daiko Electric Co Ltd

Designed in a satirical shape of a classic electric bulb, the globe houses high-tech light emitting diode (LED) lamps providing low levels of energy consumption, infinite lamp life as well as intensified point luminosity.

2002

"C.W.T. DINING" — Table
Materials: acrylic resin
Manufacturer: Waazwiz Ltd

"MASETTE" — Table
Materials: acrylic resin, walnut veneer
Manufacturer: Waazwiz Ltd

"LENORAT" — Suspension Lighting/Flower Vase (below)
Materials: acrylic resin, chrome-plated steel, LED lamps
Manufacturer: Waazwiz Ltd

Kurokawa's concept of the ultimate lighting fixture as one shedding light on the beauty of nature led to the design of this fixture which serves a dual function as a vase.

 2003

"DALFS" — Luminescent Candle
Materials: luminescent acrylic resin
Manufacturer: Waazwiz Ltd

"FALOM" — Armchair
Materials: steel, leather, fabric
Manufacturer: CASSINA IXC. Ltd

EXHIBITIONS

 1997

"H.DESIGN—FURNITURES BALANCE"
Living Design Center Ozone
Shinjuku, Tokyo

"FAVORITE.H"
Time & Style
Meguro, Tokyo

 1998

"H.DESIGN—HAPPENING"
B1 F Nowhere
Jingumae, Tokyo

 1999

"H.DESIGN"
Il Salone Satellite 1999
Milan, Italy

"H.DESIGN PRODUCTS 1999—HAPPENING"
Aoyama, Tokyo

 2000

"OUT.DeSIGN"
Salon du Meuble de Paris Design Lab
Paris, France

"OUT.DeSIGN P00DB*T" — TOKYO DESIGNERS BLOCK 2000
1F Hillside Terrace F Block
Daikanyama, Tokyo

"OUT.DeSIGN P00Ha*T—HAPPENING"
Idee Shop
Aoyama, Tokyo

 2001

"SPUTNIK"
Fuori Salone
Milan, Italy

"TSUTOMU KUROKAWA OUT.DeSIGN P01DB*T"
Batsu Art Gallery
Jingumae, Tokyo

"TOM DIXON DESIGN FACTORY"
Laforet Museum Harajuku
Jingumae, Tokyo

 2002

"TSUTOMU KUROKAWA OUT.DeSIGN P02DB*T"
Omni Q Gallery
Aoyama, Tokyo

 2003

"WAAZWIZ"
Now!>Design a Vivre
Salon du Maison et Objet
Paris, France

Yoshihiko MAMIYA

After graduating from the Art College of Kobe in 1978, Mamiya was employed by Nitten the following year and Xebec in 1981. He set up a studio in Osaka, his hometown (1989), in Tokyo (1997) and in Shanghai (2001), where he is at present managing five projects in the Chinese provinces of Shanghai, Dalian, Beijing as well as Guangdong. Mamiya lectured at the Kyoto Creative Design College and Shusei Technical College in 2001 before opening Concent—a shop that retails his furniture designs—in 2002.

BOUTIQUES, SHOPS & SHOWROOMS

 1993

45RPM
1-6-14 Nishi-shinsaibashi
Chuo-ku, Osaka

 1994

SPACE
5-5-25 Minami-aoyama
Minato-ku, Tokyo

 1995

45RPM SHIBUYA
6-19-16 Jingumae
Shibuya-ku, Tokyo

 1997

CLIO BLUE AOYAMA
5-6-25 Minami-aoyama
Minato-ku, Tokyo

DENIME (below)
1-11-21 Minami-horie
Nishi-ku, Osaka

 1998

AQUA GIRL
1-20-17 Jinnan
Shibuya-ku, Tokyo

CHIT CHAT CHOT
4-6-14 Bakuro-cho
Chuo-ku, Osaka

E&Y
4-6-14 Bakuro-cho
Chuo-ku, Osaka

DENIME
576-1 Takamiya-cho
Takoyakushi-sagaru Tomiko-ji
Nakagyo-ku, Kyoto

 1999

INDEX HARAJUKU
6-5-6 Jingumae
Shibuya-ku, Tokyo

 2000

AQUA GIRL
1-6-7 Shinsaibashi
Chuo-ku, Osaka

For the boutique specializing in precious vintage jeans, Mamiya created a harmonious interior filled with retro furnishings to complement and recall the history of the merchandise.

CLIO BLUE
2-10-15 Sannomiya
Chuo-ku, Kobe

 2001

RICHARD GINORI
1-7-1 Yurakucho
Chiyoda-ku, Tokyo

GISELE PARKER
5-2-14 Jingumae
Shibuya-ku, Tokyo

LEVI'S
4-41-1 Bakuro-cho
Chuo-ku, Osaka

 2002

LA SORTIR DU SECOURES
1-17-1 Kita-horie
Nishi-ku, Osaka

AQUA GIRL
2F Marunouchi Bldg
2-4-1 Marunouchi
Chiyoda-ku, Tokyo

AIDEC SHOWROOM
1F Tower Aoyama
2-24-15 Minami-aoyama
Minato-ku, Tokyo

HAN AHN SOON
1-17-1 Kita-horie
Nishi-ku, Osaka

GRUN
1-17-1 Kita-horie
Nishi-ku, Osaka

HAIR SALONS

 1994

DESTIJL-1
2F 1-1-1 Shinsaibashi-suji
Chuo-ku, Osaka

GLAMOUR KANSAI HAIRDRESSING
TECHNICAL COLLEGE
3-2-9 Nanba-naka
Naniwa-ku, Osaka

 1996

DEW
1-4-4 Nanba-naka
Naniwa-ku, Osaka

LIM HAIR & CAFE
4-13-11 Minami-senba
Chuo-ku, Osaka

 1997

T K IT'S HAIR
1-10-4 Nishi-shinsaibashi
Chuo-ku, Osaka

 2001

HAIR DO
3-1 Shinmachi
Chuo-ku, Chiba

DEW
4-41-1 Bakuro-cho
Chuo-ku, Osaka

 2002

FIRST NAILS
B1F Navio
7-10 Kakuta-cho
Kita-ku, Osaka

RESTAURANTS, CAFES, BARS & CLUBS

 1988

TSURUMATSU
1-3-34 Dojima
Kita-ku, Osaka

 1989

MARBLE
5F Shin Saito Bldg
1-19 Higashi-shinsaibashi
Chuo-ku, Osaka

COOC A HOOP
Empire Bldg
Sanjo-agaru, Kiya-machi
Nakagyo-ku, Kyoto

 1990

KIRIVE
B1F1-17-16 Shinano-machi
Chuo-ku, Osaka

QUIXOTIC BAR
B1F 2-9-5 Nishi-shinbashi
Chuo-ku, Osaka

 1991

CAFE BOIT QOO
1-4-4 Nanba-naka
Naniwa-ku, Osaka

 1992

KUSHI DOKORO MOGAMI
1F 1-10-16 Sonezaki-shinchi
Kita-ku, Osaka

 1993

7TH FLOOR
7F On Air West Bldg
2-3 Maruyama-cho
Shibuya-ku, Tokyo

 1994

TIINA
1-1-48 Katamachi
Miyako-jima, Osaka

 1995

KITCHEN DINE
1-6-5 Tanimachi
Chuo-ku, Osaka

 1996

CAFE COLOMBIA
2F 1-12-6 Higashi-shinsaibashi
Chuo-ku, Osaka

UN CAFE
B2F 5-53-67 Jingumae
Shibuya-ku, Tokyo

CLUB ASIA
1-8 Maruyama-cho
Shibuya-ku, Tokyo

 1997

NANANIN
4-7-3 Bakuro-cho
Chuo-ku, Osaka

NOT BLUE
2F 156 Nishiki-cho
Himeji, Hyogo Prefecture

HONEY BEE
8F Kyoto Station Bldg
Shiokoji-sagaru Karasuma-dori
Shimogyo-ku, Kyoto

 1998

FACTORY CAFE
1-14-28 Minami-horie
Nishi-ku, Osaka

HIGH CAMP QOO
3-2 Umeda
Kita-ku, Osaka

ZEPP (below)
1-18-31 Nanko-kita
Suminoe-ku, Osaka

Keeping in mind that a concert hall foyer is an auxiliary facility, Mamiya created this slick bar for thirst quenching and for sharing post-concert excitement in balance with the overall design.

 1999

OLIVE DE CAFE
1-5-24 Shinsaibashi
Chuo-ku, Osaka

OLIVE DE CAFE SENDAI
3-10-24 1-Bancho
Aoba-ku, Sendai

BIG CAT
1-6-14 Nishi-shinsaibashi
Chuo-ku, Osaka

2000

MATSURICA
1-27-9 Aoba-dai
Meguro-ku, Tokyo

NANKARO
2-1-25 Nishi-shinsaibashi
Chuo-ku, Osaka

DIINA
2F 1-1-12 Minami-horie
Nishi-ku, Osaka

 2001

E.H.BANK
9 Kaigan-dori
Chuo-ku, Kobe

REPAIR
1-11 Kamiyama-cho
Kita-ku, Osaka

DREW
1-9-9 Nishi-honmachi
Nishi-ku, Osaka

ON AIR OSAKA
2-6-20 Umeda
Kita-ku, Osaka

XINTIANDI ARK
House15, North Block
Xintiandi Lane 181,Taicang Rd
Shanghai, China

 2002

EN VUE (below)
1-17-1 Kita-horie
Nishi-ku, Osaka

The ambience of a mountain retreat was created for this French restaurant, allowing diners to forget the city noise and immerse themselves in the stillness of the mountain.

CAFE VUE
1-17-1 Kita-horie
Nishi-ku, Osaka

2ND LINE
7-11-37 Fukushima
Fukushima-ku, Osaka

LOUNGE NEO
2-12-7 Dogenzaka
Shibuya-ku, Tokyo

 2003

MITTE
2-4 Honmachi
Chuo-ku, Osaka

CLUB O
2-21-7 Dogenzaka
Shibuya-ku, Tokyo

HOTELS & INNS

 1985

PENSION NORIKURA
Norikura-kogen Azumi-mura
Minami-azumigun
Nagano Prefecture

 1991

AWAJI INTERNATIONAL HOTEL ALEX
Ohama-kaigan Dori
Sumoto, Hyogo Prefecture

 1994

MUSASHINO
90 Kasugano
Nara Prefecture

COMMERCIAL CENTERS

 1998

DRAPEAU
4-6-14 Bakuro-cho
Chuo-ku, Osaka

 2001

F-DRESS MINAMI-SENBA
4-41-1 Bakuro-cho
Chuo-ku, Osaka

 2002

COR BDLG.
1-17-1 Kita-horie
Nishi-ku, Osaka

RESIDENCES

 1997

N RESIDENCE
Kawachi-nagano, Osaka

 1998

A RESIDENCE
Kita-ku, Kobe

M RESIDENCE (below)
Sakai, Osaka

In this residence, daily activities, objects and equipment are categorized by necessity and function. Likewise, the interior architecture is free of any superfluous elements.

 2002

N RESIDENCE
Sumiyoshi-ku, Osaka

 2003

O RESIDENCE
Habikino, Osaka

Ichiro SATO

Born in Tokyo, Sato graduated from Kuwazawa Design School in 1984. He was employed by Super Potato and served as member of staff until establishing his own studio in 1994. He opened a café called "Papaya" next to his present studio in 2000. He is currently involved in the design of a large-scale Japanese restaurant in New York scheduled to open in autumn 2004.

RESTAURANTS & BARS

 1996

TSUKI NO NIWA
1-4-8 Nishi-azabu
Minato-ku, Tokyo

 1997

JIYUGAOKA GRILL
1-25-2 Nakane
Meguro-ku, Tokyo

TAMASAKA
2-21-11 Nishi-azabu
Minato-ku, Tokyo

 1998

HIGASHIYAMA TOKYO
1-21-25 Higashiyama
Meguro-ku, Tokyo

KAN
2-1-2 Higashiyama
Meguro-ku, Tokyo

TOKYO GYOZA RO
4-4-2 Taishido
Setagaya-ku, Tokyo

KONBUYA
B1F Next Nishi-azabu
4-10-5 Nishi-azabu
Minato-ku, Tokyo

2000

THE RIVER ORIENTAL
Matsubara-agaru, Kiya-cho dori
Shimogyo-ku, Kyoto

THE TOKYO RESTAURANT
2-4-1 Minami-azabu
Minato-ku, Tokyo

NANGOKU SHUKA
8F Isetan Department Store
1-11-5 Kichijoji Honmachi
Musashino-shi, Tokyo

DRAGON HALL
4-4-12 Nishi-azabu
Minato-ku,Tokyo

OOKAMADO MESHI TORAFUKU AOYAMA
B1F Aoyama Hanashige Bldg
3-12-9 Kita-aoyama
Minato-ku, Tokyo

 2001

THE HANEZAWA GARDEN
3-12-15 Hiroo
Shibuya-ku, Tokyo

THE HOUSE OF PACIFIC
1-5-10 Kitano-cho
Chuo-ku, Kobe

THE GARDEN ORIENTAL SOSHUEN
4-7-28 Sumiyoshi Yamate
Higashi-nada-ku, Kobe

CHINA DOLL
2-19-7 Kichijoji Honmachi
Musashino-shi, Tokyo

ONOHAN
7-17-2 Roppongi
Minato-ku, Tokyo

TIBET TIBET
2F Nice Bldg
5-29-9 Setagaya-ku, Tokyo

TURUKAME
2-20-7 2-16-17 Kichijoji Honmachi
Musashino-shi, Tokyo

 2002

NANGOKUSHUKA HARAJUKU HONTEN
B1F Coop Olympia
6-35-3 Jingumae
Shibuya-ku, Tokyo

AOYAMA KAWA NO HOTORI DE
B1F 2002 Bldg
5-8-5 Minami-aoyama
Minato-ku, Tokyo

TSUDA NO FUJI ZABO (below)
1-15 Nanama-cho
Shizuoka, Shizuoka Prefecture

Illuminated paper vases create a playful display in one of the many private dining rooms of this four-story, resort-style Japanese restaurant located in the provincial city of Shizuoka.

SOUP STOCK TOKYO
B1F Marunouchi Bldg
2-4-1 Marunouchi
Chiyoda-ku, Tokyo

OZASHKI TENPURA TENMASA
35 F Marunouchi Bldg
2-4-1 Marunouchi
Chiyoda-ku, Tokyo

INABA TOSHIRO
35 F Marunouchi Bldg
2-4-1 Marunouchi
Chiyoda-ku, Tokyo

THE SEAZONER FUTAKO TAMAGAWA
1F Oak Maisonette Bldg
3-20-13 Tamagawa
Setagaya-ku,Tokyo

KONAYA
B2F Caretta Shiodome
1-8-2 Higashi-shinbashi
Minato-ku, Tokyo

 2003

SHUNPU BANRI
9F Laqua Tokyo Dome City
1-1-1 Kasuga
Bunkyo-ku, Tokyo

JAPANESE CUISINE EN
42F Shiodome City Center Bldg
1-5-2 Higashi-shinbashi
Minato-ku, Tokyo

SAKAEYA KAWASAKI
La Cittadella
4-1 Ogawa-cho, Kawasaki-ku
Kawasaki, Kanagawa Prefecture

AMANDAN TERRACE
702-2 Ueda
Tenpaku-ku, Nagoya

YOUNHEY
Daichi Ginza Bldg
5-10-6 Ginza
Chuo-ku, Tokyo

JYUSEN KAZEN
7-22 Minamimachi
Shizuoka, Shizuoka Prefecture

MARUKA UDON
3-16 Ogawa-machi Kanda
Chiyoda-ku, Tokyo

ABURYANSE HYAKKANN
9F Kokubunji El
3-20-3 Minami-cho
Kokubunji-shi, Tokyo

SUSHI KYU
B1f Toshita Bldg
3-4-11 Nihonbashi
Chuo-ku, Tokyo

HIGENOUSHI / PACHA
1F-3F Minami 3-jo Nishi 5-chome
Sapporo, Hokkaido

ANTONIO'S
B1F Shin Tokyo Bldg
3-3-1 Marunouchi
Chiyoda-ku, Tokyo

ISEMON
B1F Tochigi Bldg
1-3-15 Nishi-shinjuku
Shinjuku-ku, Tokyo

SOBAYA YAMATO
3-1-17 Uehara
Shibuya-ku, Tokyo

SABUROKU
10-3 Higashi-machi
Tokorozawa, Saitama Prefecture

KUROZA AKATSUKI RO
1F Akasaka Nakagawa Bldg
3-11-3 Akasaka
Minato-ku, Tokyo

 2004

NIBANCHO RESTAURANT
3-7-15 Nibancho
Matsuyama, Ehime Prefecture

JAPANESE CUISINE EN N.Y.
435 Hudson Street
New York, New York

IZUMO KAIKAN RENEWAL PROJECT
1-61 Higashi-cho, Omiya-ku
Saitama, Saitama Prefecture

HANAZONO
The Ritz Carlton Hotel
602 Yeoksam-dong, Kangnam-gu
Seoul, Korea

204

BOUTIQUES & SHOPS

1998 ~ 2001

TAKEO KIKUCHI (below)
Hanshin Department Store
1-13-13 Umeda
Kita-ku, Osaka
(60 boutiques nationwide)

Sato's design concept for the nationwide series of boutiques for the menswear designer focused on a collapsible shelving system designed in teak and steel.

2001

OBJ EAST
2-8-9 Ginza
Chuo-ku, Tokyo

2002

KAKUNODATE SATOKU GARDEN
26 Higashi-katsuraku-cho
Kakunodate-machi
Senhoku-gun, Akita Prefecture

2003

THE SOVEREIGN HOUSE (below)
1F Shin Tokyo Bldg
3-3-1 Marunouchi
Chiyoda-ku, Tokyo

This shop, selling the most exclusive brand under the renowned retailer United Arrows, is a luxurious boutique which Sato created with a flavor of British Colonial style.

UNITED ARROWS for women
2-31-12 Jingumae
Shibuya-ku, Tokyo

SWORD FISH
4F Shibuya109
2-29-1 Dogenzaka
Shibuya-ku, Tokyo

2004

UNITED ARROWS NIHONBASHI
1F Coredo Nihonbashi
1-4-1 Nihonbashi
Chuo-ku, Tokyo

Hisanobu TSUJIMURA

Born in Kyoto and employed by Livart in 1983, Tsujimura set up his own studio in 1995 and Moon Balance—a furniture design company—in 2002. He has won many awards, including the Nashop Lighting Contest Grand Prix Award in 1977 and the JCD Design Second Award in 1997, 1998 and 1999. Currently lecturing at the Kyoto Prefectural University and Kyoto Seika University, he recently completed the design of Togetsuso Kinryu, a traditional Japanese inn which he himself had earlier renovated, but had later burnt down, and is now scheduled to re-open in 2005.

RESTAURANTS & BARS

1995

RICORDI
4F Sfera Bldg
17 Benzaiten-cho
Higashiyama-ku, Kyoto

1996

BLUE CAFE
1F New City Makishi
2-3-13 Makishi,
Naha, Okinawa Prefecture

1997

BAR MOON
5F JOY Bldg
Nijjo-kawaramachi, Nishi-kita Kado
Nakagyo-ku, Kyoto

CLOUD 9
930 Noji-cho
Kusatsu, Shiga Prefecture

RESIDENCES

2002

S HOUSE
Shibuya-ku, Tokyo

OFFICES

2002

MITSUBISHI TOKYO WEALTH MANAGEMENT
1-1-1 Uchisaiwai-cho
Chiyoda-ku, Tokyo

CHA CHA
2F Aivex Bldg
2-chome Hon-dori
Naka-ku, Hiroshima

1998

DINING CHANTO
4F Shijo Kawaramachi Bldg
Kawaramachi Shijo-sagaru
Nakagyo-ku, Kyoto

1999

MEIYACCHA
B2F TK Bldg
1-4-14 Higashi-shinsaibashi
Chuo-ku, Osaka

NOODLE+BAR
6F Asse
2-37 Matsubara-cho
Minami-ku, Hiroshima

POSITIVE EATING
2-18 Komachi
Nakai-ku, Hiroshima

BAR LOOP
B!F Acend Bldg
2-271-2 Kita-kurumaya-cho
Kawaramachi Sanjo-sagaru
Nakagyo-ku, Kyoto

2000

YUSOSHI
6F Myojo Koen Bldg
1-15-7 Jinnan
Shibuya-ku, Tokyo

BUSSARAKAN
B1 Acend Bldg
173-1 Kiyamachi Matsubara-agaru
Minoya-cho
Shimogyo-ku, Kyoto

ENOTECA RICORDI SALA V.I.P.
3F Sfera Bldg
17 Benzaiten-cho
Higashiyama-ku, Kyoto

CHA CHA SHIROGANE (below)
5-14-5 Shirogane
Minato-ku Tokyo

A soothing, modern Japanese design with light walls of hand-crafted paper was created for its effect on the Japanese subconscious of Tokyo diners.

YEN
22 rue Saint-Benoit
Paris 75006, France

KAKIYASU SHANGHAI DINING
1524-6 Oaza Moritada-aza Hiromi
Kuwana, Mie Prefecture

2001

CHANOMA MEGURO
1-22-4-6F Kami-meguro
Meguro-ku, Tokyo

CHA CHA MINAMI AOYAMA
5-9-1 Minami-aoyama
Minato-ku, Tokyo

CHA CHA HANA
1-1-1 Kabuki-cho
Shinjuku-ku, Tokyo

YUSOSHI
2F Hankyu Department Store
8-7 Kakuta-cho
Kita-ku, Osaka

HINANO
1F Kenji Bldg
1-3106 Seiwa
Fukui, Fukui Prefecture

CHANDELEUR
1+2F Kenji Bldg
1-3106 Seiwa
Fukui, Fukui Prefecture

YUSOSHI + CODOMO SHOW
5F Moon B Bldg
378 Kameya-cho Gokomachi-dori
Oike-agaru
Nakagyo-ku, Kyoto

CHANOMA
Akara Renga Soko Bldg 2
Naka-ku, Yokohama

ISHIBEKOJI MAMECHA
7F Yokohama Lumine
2-16-1 Takashima
Nishi-ku, Yokohama

ISHIBEKOJI MAMECHA
Ishibekoji Minami-mon-sagaru
Yasakajinjya
Higashiyama-ku, Kyoto

TENSHA
B1 Hillside
6-10-1 Roppongi
Minato-ku, Tokyo

KAGAYA SHOKUDO
2083 Sayada
Kumagaya, Saitama Prefecture

BOUTIQUES & SHOPS

OPTIQUE NIWAKA
401 Shimomaruya-cho Kawaramachi
Oike-sagaru
Nakagyo-ku, Kyoto

NIWAKA
64 Broome Street
New York, New York 10012

IRREGULAR VERB PLUS+
1F P-91 Bldg
Shinkyogoku Shijo-agaru Nakano-cho
Nakagyo-ku, Kyoto

MOTORWN
1F Minami-senba DS Bldg
3-6-3 Minami-senba
Chuo-ku, Osaka

GALLERY YUI
1F Ground Hills Okazaki Jingumichi
91 Enshoji-cho, Okazaki
Sakyo-ku, Kyoto

OTHERS TO COLORS + TEA (below)
341-2 Oritate
Gifu, Gifu Prefecture

An illuminated line running along the perimeter of the boutique and café accentuates the clean white, minimalist design.

TEEMS DESIGN + MOON BALANCE
3F Moon B Bldg
378 Kameya-cho Gokomachi-dori
Oike-sagaru
Nakagyo-ku, Kyoto

D+M
2F Venus Fort Palette Town
1-chome Aomi
Koto-ku, Tokyo

LAB LABO
2F Venus Fort Palette Town
1-chome Aomi
Koto-ku, Tokyo

LUCIE
Sanjo-dori Yanaginobanba
Minami-nishi-kado
Nakagyo-ku, Kyoto

CHANGES UNITED ARROWS
1F Matsuzakaya Department Store
3-16-1 Sakae
Naka-ku, Nagoya

HAIR SALONS

KUN KUN LU HO
2F Noa Bldg
Higashinotoin Nishikikoji-agaru
Nakagyo-ku, Kyoto

CUT & PARM CURL
1F Kagmura Bldg
Higashinotoin Nishi-koji-agaru
Nakagyo-ku, Kyoto

KUN KUN LU HO
2F Shinyu Bldg
268-1 Nakahakusan-cho
Fuyacho-oike
Nakagyo-ku, Kyoto

KUN KUN LU HO
390-1 Koya-cho
Sakaimachi-dori Rokkaku-sagaru
Nakagyo-ku, Kyoto

EXHIBITIONS

"MAYU"
Idee Shop
Aoyama, Tokyo

"EXIST"
Livart Shop
Kyoto

"FURNITURES OF TSUJIMURA HISANOBU"
Living Design Center Ozone Gallery
Shinjuku, Tokyo

"ZAISU—A SHEET OF" —
TOKYO DESIGNERS WEEK CHAIR EXHIBITION
Herbert von Karajan Platz in Ark Hills
Akasaka, Tokyo

"NOW YOU SEE IT...(NOW YOU DON'T)" —
TOKYO DESIGNERS BLOCK 2001
Idee Shop
Aoyama, Tokyo

"EXPERIMENTAL FURNITURE...ON A COIL" —
TOKYO DESIGNERS WEEK FURNITURE EXHIBITION
Herbert von Karajan Platz in Ark Hills
Akasaka, Tokyo

"WA-QU EXHIBITION"
Kaigan-dori Gallery Caso
Osaka

2003

"WA-QU EXHIBITION—JAPANESE CREATION IN MILANO"
East End Studio
Milan, Italy

"SOU-SOU" —
TOKYO DESIGNERS WEEK
CONTAINER EXHIBITION
Aomi, Tokyo

"CHABU-DAI" —
TOKYO DESIGNERS WEEK
TABLE EXHIBITION
Herbert von Karajan Platz in Ark Hills
Akasaka, Tokyo

OTHERS

1998

TOGETSUSO KINRYU — Traditional Inn
916-1 Syuzenji Syuzenji-cho
Takata-gun, Shizuoka Prefecture

2002

DAISHI-JI — Buddhist Temple
(below)
2-14-1 Mino
Mino-shi, Osaka

This beautiful gold-embellished room, here bathed in an immaculate, serene light, was designed by Tsujimura to honor the ashes of the dead resting in the charnel of the Daishi-ji Temple.

2003

TESHIMA RYOKAN — Inn
Genga, Ajisu-cho
Yoshiki-gun, Yamaguchi Prefecture

PRODUCTS

1996

"PEANUTS CHAIR" — Chair
Materials: fabric, aluminum
Manufacturer: Icon Moon Balance

"FLOAT TABLE" — Table
Materials: walnut, glass
Manufacturer: Icon Moon Balance

"PC TABLE" — Nesting Tables
Materials: melamine, plywood, aluminum
Manufacturer: Icon Moon Balance

"HAT STAND" — Hat Stand
Materials: aluminum
Manufacturer: Icon Moon Balance

1999

"MAKE DIM" — Sofa
Materials: fabric, aluminum
Manufacturer: Icon Moon Balance

"EBONY & IVORY" — Chair
Materials: beech
Manufacturer: Asplund Co Ltd

"KO-MO-RE-BI" — Series of Chairs
Materials: wicker, beech
Manufacturer: Asplund Co Ltd

"TU" — Series of Chairs
Materials: fabric, maple, beech
Manufacturer: Asplund Co Ltd

"ELEPHANT" — Sofa
Materials: wicker, steel
Manufacturer: Asplund Co Ltd

2001

"STAMP CHAIR" — Chair
Materials: stainless, elastic
Manufacturer: Pour Annick

"STAMP TABLE" — Table
Materials: rosewood, stainless
Manufacturer: Pour Annick

"SKIP" — Chair and Bar Chair
Materials: fabric, stainless
Manufacturer: Asplund Co Ltd

2002

"CUSHION TABLE" — Table with Cushions
Materials: rosewood, fabric, stainless
Manufacturer: Icon Moon Balance

"PUT MAN"— Ottoman
Materials: fabric, steel silver
Manufacturer: Icon Moon Balance

"ROUND BOX"— Cabinet
Materials: paulownia, felt
Manufacturer: Icon Moon Balance

"WRAP STOOL" — Chair (below)
Materials: titanium
Manufacturer: Icon Moon Balance

The points of two conical forms were fused to create this futuristic stool, fabricated in purple titanium and manufactured by the designer's furniture company.

"KARAMERU-S" — Cushion
Materials: leather
Manufacturer: Icon Moon Balance

2003

"HOP" — Chair
Materials: fabric, plywood
Manufacturer: Asplund Co Ltd

"PLOT" — Chair
Materials: leather
Manufacturer: Asplund Co Ltd

"PAS" — Armchair
Materials: wicker, steel, fabric
Manufacturer: Asplund Co Ltd

"CLIP" — Chair
Materials: wicker, steel, fabric
Manufacturer: Asplund Co Ltd

"PEEP" — Chair
Materials: abaca, steel, fabric
Manufacturer: Asplund Co Ltd

"WRAP" — Stool
Materials: leather, steel
Manufacturer: Asplund Co Ltd

"TSUBURI" — Stool
Materials: leather, fabric
Manufacturer: Asplund Co Ltd

"RIN" — Armchair and Chair
Materials: white ash, fabric
Manufacturer: Aidec Co Ltd

I would like to thank the following people for their kind support:

Minako Fujisawa of Fumita Design Office
Kayo Kimura of Infix Design
Wakana Miyashiro of Age
Sarah Oh of Periplus Editions
Koichi Torimura of Nacasa & Partners
Shigeru Yoshimura of Hisanobu Tsujimura Design Office

DESIGNERS

Akihito FUMITA
Fumita Design Office Inc

Address: IF+B1F Fukuda Bldg
2-8-12 Minami Aoyama
Minato-ku, Tokyo 107-0062
Tel: [81-3] 5414-2880
E-mail: info@fumitadesign.com
URL: www.fumitadesign.com

Photography
Nacasa & Partners
Seiryo Yamada (NATURAL BODY)

Takao KATSUTA
Line Inc

Address: 2F Kazami Bldg
1-1-6 Higashiyama
Meguro-ku, Tokyo 153-0043
Tel: [81-3] 5773-3536
E-mail: line@line-inc.co.jp

Photography
Kozo Takayama

Yoshihiko MAMIYA
Infix Design Incorporated

Osaka Office
Address: 3F Laid Bldg
1-9-9 Nishi-honmachi
Nishi-ku, Osaka 550-0005
Tel: [81-6] 6110-1128
E-mail: info@infix-design.com
URL: www.infix-design.com

Tokyo Office
Address: 3F 5-50-6 Jingumae
Shibuya-ku, Tokyo 150-0001
Tel: [81-3] 5468-5700

Shanghai Office
Address: 602A 28 Bldg Xintiandi
119 Madang Rd
Shanghai, China
Tel: [86-21] 6387-7252

Photography
Nacasa & Partners
Seiryo Yamada (MUSE and /SCRUB)

Yukio HASHIMOTO
Hashimoto Yukio Design Co Ltd

Address: 4-2-5 Sendagaya
Shibuya-ku, Tokyo 151-0051
Tel: [81-3] 5474-1724
E-mail: hydesign@din.or.jp
URL: www.din.or.jp/~hydesign

Photography
Nacasa & Partners
Yoichi Nagano (GEKKA)

Tsutomu KUROKAWA
Out Design Co Ltd

Address: 2-3-2 Kami-osaki
Shingawa-ku, Tokyo 141-0021
Tel: [81-3] 5789-0202
E-mail: info@outdesign.com
URL: www.outdesign.com

Photography
Kozo Takayama

Ichiro SATO
Age Co Ltd

Address: #102 2-19-8 Tomigaya
Shibuya-ku, Tokyo 151-0063
Tel: [81-3] 5738-1031
E-mail: koho@age-co.biz
URL: www.age-co.biz

Photography
Nacasa & Partners

Hisanobu TSUJIMURA
Hisanobu Tsujimura Design Office
+ Moon Balance Co Ltd

Address: 378 Kameya-cho
Gokomachi, Oike-agaru
Nakagyo-ku, Kyoto 604-0941
Tel: [81-75] 221-6403
E-mail: vc3h-tjmr@asahi-net.or.jp
URL: www.tsujimura-hisanobu.com

Photography
Nacasa & Partners
Kozo Takayama (CHA CHA 3 LOTUS)

Published by: Periplus Editions
with editorial offices at
130 Joo Seng Road #06-01
Singapore 368357

Book Design by: Sai Co Ltd
#1401 Jingumae Cooprus
6-25-8 Jingumae
Shibuya-ku, Tokyo 150-001
Tel: [81-3] 5485-1917
E-mail: sai-1@pluto.dti.ne.jp

Photography by: Nacasa & Partners Inc
3-5-5 Minami-azabu
Minato-ku, Tokyo 106-0047
Tel: [81-3] 3444-2922
E-mail: partners@nacasa.co.jp

Kozo Takayama
#402 1-1-64 Naka-meguro
Meguro-ku, Tokyo 153-0061
Tel: [81-3] 5724-5051
E-mail: kozo@mxt.mesh.ne.jp

Seiryo Yamada
3-2-9 Tenman
Kita-ku, Osaka 530-0043
Tel: [81-6] 6357-0897

Yoichi Nagano
3F 2-6-18 Jingumae
Shibuya-ku, Tokyo 150-0001
Tel: [81-3] 5772-9028
E-mail: yoyo@siren.ocn.ne.jp

Distributed by:

*North America,
Latin America and Europe*
Tuttle Publishing
364 Innovation Drive
North Clarendon, VT 05759-9436
Tel: [802] 773-8930
Fax: [802] 773-6993
E-mail: info@tuttlepublishing.com
www.tuttlepublishing.com

Japan
Tuttle Publishing
3F Yaekari Bldg
5-4-12 Osaki, Shinagawa-ku
Tokyo 141-0032, Japan
Tel: [81-3] 5437-0171
Fax: [81-3] 5437-0755
E-mail: tuttle-sales@gol.com

Asia Pacific
Berkeley Books Pte Ltd
130 Joo Seng Road #06-01
Singapore 368357
Tel: [65] 6280-1330
Fax: [65] 6280-6290
E-mail: inquiries@periplus.com.sg